Professional Issues in Primary Practice

16

Professional Issues in Primary Practice

PGCE Professional Workbooks

Titles in the series:

Professional Issues in Primary Practice
ISBN: 1 903300 65 7
Price: £14

Primary ICT
ISBN: 1 903300 64 9
Price: £14

Primary English
ISBN: 1 903300 61 4
Price: £14

Primary Mathematics
ISBN: 1 903300 62 2
Price: £14

Primary Science
ISBN: 1 903300 63 0
Price: £14

Foundation Stage
ISBN: 1 903300 67 3
Price: £14

To order, please contact our distributors:

Plymbridge Distributors
Estover Road
Plymouth PL6 7PY
Tel: 01752 202301
Fax: 01752 202333
Email: orders@plymbridge.com
www.plymbridge.com

Emma Asprey, Cathy Hamilton and Susan Haywood

PGCE Professional Workbook

Professional Issues in Primary Practice

www.learningmatters.co.uk

First published in 2002 by Learning Matters Ltd.

British Library Cataloguing in Publication Data
A CIP record for this book is available from the British Library.

ISBN 1 903300 65 7

Cover design by Topics – The Creative Partnership
Project management by Deer Park Productions
Typeset by Sparks Computer Solutions Ltd – www.sparks.co.uk
Printed and bound in Great Britain by Ashford Colour Press, Gosport, Hants

Learning Matters Ltd
58 Wonford Road
Exeter EX2 4LQ
Tel: 01392 215560
Email: info@learningmatters.co.uk
www.learningmatters.co.uk

Contents

Chapter 1   General introduction

Initial teacher training

Initial teacher training is the start of a continuing process, designed to support your professional development throughout your teaching career. This book will support you in identifying strengths and areas for further development, and help you meet the Professional Standards for the award of Qualified Teacher Status (QTS). These Standards set out what a trainee teacher must know, understand and be able to do to be awarded QTS. You will find them listed on the Teacher Training Agency (TTA) website at www.canteach.gov.uk

There are a variety of different training routes into primary teaching. This book is designed to be flexible enough to support trainees studying on a range of routes but particularly those working on employment-based, flexible, modular or part-time PGCE courses. Trainees on full-time PGCE courses should also find it a useful resource.

Providing a combination of theoretical study and practical experiences it is intended to give you the opportunity to develop as a reflective and critical practitioner. You will need to develop a strong theoretical foundation to your work and learn to critically analyse your own practice, as well as understand the social and political context within which schools operate, in order to develop skills that will help you become an effective teacher.

Content of this book

We believe that successful primary teachers:

⊃ are committed to teaching;
⊃ are flexible, creative, innovative, imaginative, confident, critically aware and open minded;
⊃ use a range of teaching styles and strategies which draw upon a theoretical knowledge base which informs all aspects of their practice;
⊃ appreciate individuality, value diversity and are able to collaborate;
⊃ believe in the need to be lifelong learners.

It is on the basis of these beliefs that we have selected the following key aspects of primary professional practice as the focus of this book:

⊃ How do you define yourself in the role of the teacher?
⊃ How do children learn and teachers teach?
⊃ How do you create a learning environment?
⊃ How do you plan for learning and teaching?
⊃ How do you assess and record children's learning?
⊃ One school for all?

Of course, there are other important aspects of primary teaching which could have been given greater weighting or covered in more detail within this kind of training resource. The expectation is that trainees using this book will draw upon a range of other literature; suggestions for further reading are included to help you with this. Your training provider or other colleagues may recommend additional literature which enhances this theoretical base.

This book will provide you with the tools you need to become a competent and professional practitioner. How you engage with the process will determine the *qualitative* nature of the practitioner you will become. Your commitment, enthusiasm, expectations, aspirations, self-awareness and quest for learning are essential elements of this developmental process. As trainee teachers, you bring a wide range of valuable life experiences and prior learning which will enrich your studies. This will also support your development as a teacher who will contribute to the education of children in a changing and diverse society.

Structure of this book

In order to recognise the variety of experiences and learning with which trainees start their courses, a flexible needs assessment process is an integral part of this book. We recommend that all trainees read each theme covered in Chapter 2, which is designed to provide an introduction to each of the themes covered in the book. Each theme has a linked needs analysis and detailed guidance on using this can be found on **page 3**. Completing the needs analysis for each theme will help to inform your starting point for learning. In the first instance, however, you will need to decide on the best approach to adopt, in discussion with your teacher and training provider, based on the particular training route you are following.

Once you have read Chapter 2 and completed the needs analysis process, you will have a better idea of your strengths and areas for further development, and where to begin your learning for each theme in Chapters 3, 4 and 5. These chapters are structured around school-based activities, which can be carried out in your school placements with different age groups. Given that they are related to your general professional practice, they can be completed within different subject teaching. It is sensible to discuss your starting points for learning with your training provider and teacher before beginning any of the activities.

Once you have completed the appropriate activities in Chapters 3, 4 and 5, you may find it useful to go back to Chapter 2 and the needs analysis tables to check that you have the appropriate evidence to audit your progress against the Standards.

Whilst reading through each chapter, you will come across margin icons that represent key features of the book.

 some further reading   an example

 a cross-reference   an activity

Professional Standards for Qualified Teacher Status

By the end of your course, irrespective of the training route you have followed, you will need to demonstrate that you have met all the Standards required for the award of Qualified Teacher Status. The Standards relating to Professional Issues are detailed in the Appendix and cross-referenced to each theme covered in the book. You will be able to use the evidence gained from completing the reading and activities outlined in this book to demonstrate that you have met *some* of the Standards relating to professional practice. However, you will also need to develop a manageable but comprehensive profiling system which enables you to track your progress against *all* the Standards. Other sources of evidence include feedback from school placements as well as from your training course.

We hope you find this book a useful resource to support your training and development as a primary teacher. You are beginning a complex and lengthy journey, during which you will learn a great deal from a variety of sources, but most especially from the children with whom you will have the opportunity to work. They will provide you with the greatest challenge, laughter and delight as you seek to understand, inspire and teach them.

Guidance and needs analysis ⇒
Introduction

Contents

This chapter introduces the key professional aspects of primary teaching which are taken as themes throughout this book. The understanding of each of these themes will support you as you train and become a reflective primary teacher.

You may choose to read this chapter as a whole. Alternatively, you may choose to select specific themes that you feel are particularly relevant or important for you to consider at this time. Each theme is followed by a needs analysis table (see below for an outline of the needs analysis process). You should use the needs analysis to make a judgement about your level of professional development in relation to each theme.

The needs analysis process
Following each theme is a needs analysis to work through at your own pace, whenever you decide to audit a particular aspect of your professional understanding and practice.

Start with the column entitled 'Getting Started' and read each of the descriptor statements listed in that column. For each one, decide whether you match the descriptor and if so provide a date and evidence for your own records of having completed that particular element. If you do not feel confident that you can provide evidence for that descriptor, leave the evidence cell empty at this stage. Continue this process until you have considered each of the descriptor statements in the first column. If you have any evidence cells empty in the Getting Started column, it would be helpful to complete the activities contained in the matching theme at the Getting Started level (Chapter 3, **pages 41-63**). You will notice that some cells do not contain a descriptor. This is because the table has been constructed to demonstrate progression across the rows in the needs analysis matrix. This is not always appropriate and therefore some descriptor cells will remain empty.

Now carry out the same process in the next column entitled 'Developing your Skills' and again in the 'Extending your Skills' column.

Having read and completed the activities in the relevant sections in Chapters 3, 4 and 5, you will then need to return to the outstanding or empty evidence cells and complete these appropriately. You may find it easier to do this theme by theme, chapter by chapter, rather than leave it until you reach the end of the book.

Below is an example of a needs analysis table with some evidence filled in. We recommend that you photocopy the tables and enlarge them to A3 in order to make them easier to fill in. In this case, a trainee has started to audit herself on 'How do you create a learning environment?'. You will notice that different types of evidence can be used. These could include:

- classroom observations of other teachers' practice;
- previous experience directly related to the theme;
- examples of your own practice;
- evidence from observations by teachers;
- self-evaluations;
- reading.

Getting Started	Date/evidence	Developing your Skills	Date/evidence	Extending your Skills	Date/evidence
I am aware of the necessity for clear rules and routines in the classroom.	I have listed the rules and routines that the class are familiar with. 12.09.01	When working with the whole class I can use a range of strategies to ensure that transition periods are smooth and do not disrupt learning.	I have moved children one table at a time to line up for lunch. I have also used birthday months and other strategies to organise the class during transition periods. 4.01.02	I am aware of and can adopt the whole school policy for behaviour management consistently.	Feedback from my teacher confirmed I had demonstrated that I was using the school behaviour management policy consistently. 15.05.02
As a result of teaching individuals and small groups I can identify which rules and routines have worked best for me.	I have used a variety of strategies modelled by the teacher, evaluated these and feel confident about which I can use in different situations. For example, in an art lesson I praised children who used the materials properly. 20.10.01				
When teaching a group of children I can use established routines effectively.	I have worked with a group of children to establish rules about how the group will operate. 23.11.01	I can stop the class and gain their attention when necessary.	I have tried two or three ways of stopping the class and now use the words 'Listen please' in a clear, calm voice. The children respond to this with occasional reminders. 19.02.02		

It is quite possible that through this auditing and needs analysis process you will discover that you need to work on different themes at different levels and this could be an appropriate approach for you to adopt – for example, 'how children learn and teachers teach' at the Getting Started level but 'how to create a learning environment' at the Developing Skills level. However, you may prefer to work more systematically through each level and address each theme in turn before moving onto the next level. The book is constructed to provide this kind of flexibility in its use so that it can meet the needs of different trainees.

Chapter 2 How do you define yourself in the role of the teacher?

This section explores what it means to be a teacher and the influences which may affect you both personally and professionally. The process of becoming a teacher is outlined. This is extended to include an exploration of the ways in which you will continue to develop once you are teaching. The importance of relationships is emphasised and methods of effective communication are introduced. In this section you will be exploring:

- the reasons for becoming a teacher;
- establishing yourself as a teacher;
- your continuing development as a professional teacher.

Why do you want to teach?

There are many reasons why people want to become teachers. There is the immense satisfaction in knowing that you are making a difference to people's lives. There is the stimulation and enjoyment of working with children. There is the enthusiasm for sharing and developing understanding. There is the constant challenge of change and unpredictability. These, and many other aspects of teaching, require the teacher to have certain characteristics and skills. These are not magical attributes, they are techniques and strategies that can be learned and continually improved.

Teaching is not about knowing everything and imparting it to children. It is about encouraging and supporting children on the way to becoming independent lifelong learners, facilitating stimulating learning experiences and providing social and emotional contexts in which children can flourish.

How do you establish yourself as the teacher?

Children are at the centre of teachers' professional priorities (Moyles 1992). This gives rise to a wide range of other considerations such as relationships, organisation, planning and assessment, to name just a few. Every aspect of being a teacher draws on both your professional and personal resources and values. There is a delicate balance to be struck which allows you to build respectful relationships with children, parents and colleagues, whilst remaining objective enough to cope with setbacks (Moyles and Robinson 2002).

The way you work with children and adults will be affected to a large degree by your own beliefs, perceptions and hopes for the future. It is therefore vital that you know in your own mind what your goals and expectations are and that you maintain open and flexible attitudes. This will help you to develop an analytical approach to your teaching and to learn from critical reflection on your experiences.

The priorities of teachers could be perceived as divided into two main areas:

Relationships and holistic development	Strategy and structure
Independence	Rules
Responsibility	Routines
Confidence	Curriculum content
Self-esteem	Assessment
Creativity	Target setting
Collaboration	Standards

These areas are inextricably linked rather than mutually exclusive. Perhaps their interdependence is at the heart of effective teaching (Hayes 1999). Learning requires organisation and structure, but also relies upon knowledge of the children, their personalities and strengths. Teaching is far more complex than delivering curriculum content. Indeed learning, in the formal sense, will not take place if children do not feel emotionally confident and secure. Therefore becoming a teacher is far more complex than learning a series of simple procedures, like driving a car or using a computer. Again, these aspects of teaching will be affected by your attitudes.

How do you continue to develop as a professional teacher?

A school is a 'learning community' (Fisher 1995, Chapter 10) made up of people and built upon respectful relationships between all its members. Learning requires children to take risks, therefore the learning environment must be one in which they feel safe, secure and confident. Teachers are role models for the children they teach. Teachers who are supportive, positive, creative and challenging can help children to set high expectations for themselves and others within a caring atmosphere of autonomous learning and self-respect.

Example: *Reshma has just moved to a new school. She is a shy child, used to sitting quietly in the classroom and listening to others. During a mathematics lesson the teacher asks the class: 'What is 3 times 3?' Reshma is good at multiplication but listens to others' contributions and does not volunteer an answer. She hears the teacher praising others' efforts, whether the answer is correct or not. Eventually she raises her hand and answers a question. The teacher smiles and congratulates her on both her correct answer and being brave enough to join in on her first day in the class. With further praise and encouragement, Reshma learns that she has much to contribute and nothing to lose by attempting to answer even the most challenging questions.*

Trainee teachers often want children to like them. This is understandable but is a rather simplistic view of a complex relationship. The vital element required in a successful teacher-child relationship is mutual respect. This requires the teacher to retain a suitable detachment and objectivity in order to maintain a professional but caring approach. Simply being friendly to children will not help to maintain order or facilitate learning. It requires a far more complex combination of firmness, fairness, trustworthiness, humour and approachability. This respectful relationship will take time to develop over a number of weeks and should be monitored and nurtured constantly, never taken for granted.

Theories of development have focused on children's ability to learn and develop naturally. If we accept this to be the case, what then is the role of the teacher? Certainly, the teacher is responsible for ensuring that children's innate curiosity is not curtailed or damaged. The curriculum, with all its historical and political emphases and undercurrents, can be taught successfully only if teachers are able to channel children's energies into exploring and investigating its content. The teacher must get to know the personalities of the children in the class and how to facilitate exciting and stimulating learning experiences for each of them. To be successful in this, teachers must build on children's knowledge, understanding and experiences from outside school rather than deny the existence or belittle these important elements.

Example: *Daniel is seven years old. He is lively and has a wide range of interests, especially physical activities. During his three years at school so far he has not excelled at reading, but makes up for this by speaking articulately and explaining his ideas clearly. He has not fallen far behind his peers, but the teacher is concerned about his apparent lack of interest in books.*

During a history project, the class investigate the Vikings and their explorations. Daniel develops a fascination with finding out about people in the past and frequently brings in information from the Internet and images from magazines. His interest continues long after the class work on history has ended. The teacher decides to read Tom's Midnight Garden *to the class. Daniel is immediately gripped by the mysterious story and Tom's ability to travel back in time.*

On Monday, at the end of the day, the class are seated on the carpet waiting for the next instalment of the story. Daniel is holding his own copy of the book, bought over the weekend, and is following the story as it is read aloud. When he has finished reading the book, he starts to look for other historical stories and finds that there are several on the shelf in the classroom. His reading improves steadily, fired by his interest and growing success. His parents and teacher tell him how well he is reading.

The most productive classrooms are those in which there are open systems of communication – everyone knows what is happening and why. Expectations for learning and behaviour are made clear at the start of every lesson and the children are involved in setting the rules and limitations. Different forms of communication are used appropriately to ensure all children are included and able to contribute and there is a purposeful working atmosphere. The first meeting with a new class, for trainees and experienced teachers, is an opportunity to ensure that these systems of open communication are established early in the relationship.

Pollard (1997) describes the need for language skills, social skills and cognitive capacity (subject knowledge) in order for children and teachers to communicate in an educational context. He also outlines other non-verbal forms of communication and reminds us that these can confuse children as well as enhance their understanding. Children do not always understand what we intend to communicate. It is vital to let children express what they have understood in order to confirm their comprehension and inform the teacher of their perceptions.

Trainees need to develop a range of verbal communication skills, including exposition, question and answer exchanges, discussions and listening (Pollard 1997). This is further developed on **page 73**. Perhaps more importantly, a good teacher will know when to use each of these, or a range, to suit the task in hand. As well as matching the method of communication to the content of the learning, it should also suit the way the children are grouped for an activity.

Interactions with individuals engaged in learning activities tend to be discursive and involve listening carefully to the child to establish the precise nature of misconceptions and provide appropriate assistance. Interactions with groups of children can vary enormously according to the nature of the group. A group of children with similar learning needs may require the explanation of a task specially adapted to them, followed by questions, answers and discussion. A group of children with different strengths or learning styles, working on a practical task, may need encouragement to collaborate and discuss their ideas, thus allowing the teacher to elicit their levels of understanding. Whole class interactions are often about exposition, instructions and questions. A 'one to many' communication is best used for dissemination of information, although larger scale discussions can be very productive if carefully managed.

Example: *During the mental/oral section of a daily mathematics lesson, the teacher uses quick-fire questions to test the children's recall of multiplication facts. Questions are aimed at individuals or small groups and are differentiated to provide challenge with a good chance of success.*

During a history lesson the children assume the roles of archaeologists, digging for evidence in carefully marked-out trays of soil. Any finds must be carefully drawn and their position recorded. There is much discussion about the mystery objects, what they are made of, what their functions might have been and to whom they might have belonged. The teacher gathers the children together at the end of the lesson and lets them describe what they found and explore their theories.

You are now ready to complete the needs analysis linked to this theme in order to know how you might best proceed with your learning.

Assessment

How far have you developed your understanding of the role of the teacher? Reflect on the needs analysis table below and if possible discuss your ideas and your evidence with a colleague, teacher or tutor.

Getting Started	Date/ evidence	Developing your Skills	Date/ evidence	Extending your Skills	Date/ evidence
I have observed the number and nature of interactions between teacher and children.		I can identify the ways in which the teacher communicates approval and disapproval to the class and individuals.		I have carried out an audit of the roles and responsibilities I have undertaken in school and cross-referenced these to the TTA Standards for the Award of Qualified Teacher Status.	
I can identify ways in which the interactions relate to children's learning.		I communicate clear expectations for learning and behaviour in every lesson.			
		I celebrate achievement of expectations with individuals and groups.			
I am able to plan for and evaluate my self-presentation during a first meeting with a group of children.				I can identify the advantages and responsibilities associated with working as a member of a partnership/team.	
I can plan for and teach group work which encourages participation.		I have used and evaluated a range of techniques for building children's self-esteem through my teaching.			
		I am able to plan for the increased involvement of individuals and provide support for less confident children.			
I can identify which children participate in group interactions.					
I have informed the teacher of past experiences and achievements during school placements.					
I am able to reflect on my experiences and contribute to a weekly review meeting.		I have set three targets for my own achievements each week, based on lesson evaluations and reflection on my progress.			
		I am able to relate my weekly targets to the TTA Standards for the Award of Qualified Teacher Status.			
		I have read and understood school policy on parental partnership.		I have prepared for and met with parents to discuss children's progress.	
		I am familiar with the teacher's routines involving parents.			
				I have planned for the effective use of other adults in the classroom and provided guidance for them.	
If one or more of these is not yet ticked, you may find it helpful to complete the activities on pages 43–46.		*If one or more of these is not yet ticked, you may find it helpful to complete the activities on pages 67–70.*		*If one or more of these is not yet ticked, you may find it helpful to complete the activities on pages 99–102.*	

Chapter 2 — How do children learn and teachers teach?

Gaining an insight into how children learn will be a vital part of your development as a trainee teacher. This section will help you understand theories of learning in the classroom context. It will introduce major theories of learning and discuss the influence of these on learning styles and teaching approaches. As you begin your work in the classroom it will be important for you to recognise the impact of these theoretical frameworks on learning, teaching and curriculum development in recent years. This section will cover:

- gaining an insight into the debates on teaching and learning;
- behaviourism;
- constructivism and social constructivism;
- National Curriculum, National Literacy and Numeracy Strategies;
- the work of Howard Gardner and multiple intelligences.

Gaining an insight into the debates on teaching and learning

This section will consider the relationship between theories of learning and classroom practice.

From the second half of the last century, theories of learning have been dominated by two contrasting approaches. The earliest of these, behaviourism, is associated with the names of Skinner and Thorndike. More recently, constructivist and social constructivist theories have influenced approaches in British primary schools. These theories of learning have been developed by Piaget, Vygotsky and Bruner. These researchers often worked within the context of experimental psychology, but their findings have been taken up by educationalists and applied to the classroom in order to help understand how children learn and how teaching can be made more effective. Sometimes educationalists have taken theories and applied them to particular areas of education. For example, Seymour Papert (1993) worked with Piaget and has applied constructivist theories to understanding how children can learn more effectively using information and communication technology.

Most recently, research into the development of the brain, and work on different models of learning such as multiple intelligences and preferred sensory systems, have also influenced approaches to teaching. In some schools the development of 'accelerated learning' has drawn extensively on this research and theories connected with how we learn.

These aspects of theories of learning will now be explored in further detail.

Behaviourism

Behaviourism is based on the premise that children build up links between their experience, thinking and behaviour. Behaviour which is reinforced with praise, success or positive feedback will be repeated; behaviour which is not reinforced and which results in failure or negative feedback will be eliminated. Characteristically, the learner is seen as passive, learning is directed by the teacher and involves content which is coherent, organised and logically structured. It relies on the subject knowledge and direct teaching skills of the teacher and is suited to large groups. This teaching may not easily connect with the child's learning, existing knowledge or understanding of the world. One criticism of behaviourist approaches is that learning may be fragmented and superficial.

Example: *Kharul is practising spellings based on the 'look, cover, write, check' method. He looks at a word for a few seconds, covers it and then tries to write the same word. He checks his spelling against the original. If it is correct he goes on to the next word. If not, he repeats the exercise.*

Constructivism and social constructivism

Constructivist theories have drawn on the work of Jean Piaget (1926–1961), although he was concerned with development rather than learning. Constructivism holds that the child builds understanding through the interaction between thought and experience. With each new experience the child moves from his or her current understanding to construct new learning.

Piaget outlined four stages of development:

➲ the sensorimotor stage from birth to two years;
➲ pre-operational stage from two to seven;
➲ concrete operations from seven to eleven;
➲ formal (or abstract) operations from the age of twelve onwards.

In the first three stages the child is understood to be using direct experience of the world, through play or exploration, to develop or construct new understanding. Only when the child reaches the fourth stage does learning become more formal or abstract.

At each of these stages, *Piaget* describes development as a three-part process. A child undergoing a new experience attempts to make sense of this in the light of his or her current knowledge. This process is called 'assimilation'. If assimilation is not possible, the child will adapt or restructure knowledge based on this new experience, a process termed 'accommodation'. Resolving the conflict between the child's current and new understanding, and in so doing constructing new knowledge, results in a process of 'equilibration'. A brief reading exploring Piaget's ideas is included in Pollard (1996, Section 6.3).

Constructivist theories build on this work. Applied to the classroom, child-centred teaching approaches are characteristic of this theory, and these became influential in British classrooms following the Plowden Report into primary education published in 1967. Pollard (1996, Section 7.6) contains an extract from the Plowden Report. Constructivism recognises that the context in which learning and teaching take place is highly significant and that relationships are also fundamental to this learning process. The classroom is likely to be varied and stimulating; motivation, interest, relevance and cohesive learning are central but the role of the teacher in the child's learning may be undervalued. This approach is meaningful for the child but may underestimate his or her intellectual abilities. In the constructivist view the child is seen as an independent, active builder of his or her own understanding.

Example: *Anna is playing with water in an early years setting, and is clearly experimenting by placing different objects into the water. Some objects float and some sink. When asked by an adult helper why this happens, Anna offers an explanation such as 'it stays up because it's little' or 'it sinks because it's got holes in'. She is beginning to construct understanding based on her experience.*

Social constructivism, associated with Vygotsky and Bruner (1986), acknowledges much more explicitly the social context of learning, especially the role of language in learning. Vygotsky, whose work dates from the 1930s but was translated from the original Russian only in the 1970s, emphasises the social context in which learning takes place and the contribution of other people's intervention in the learning process.

One aspect of Vygotsky's work which is widely referred to in education is the idea of the Zone of Proximal Development. This asserts that a child working alone will reach a certain level of understanding. With the intervention of skilful and knowledgeable others, however, the child is capable of reaching a higher level of understanding. The distance between these two levels is the Zone of Proximal Development or ZPD. The intervention can come from a skilled teacher, prompting or questioning, from discussion amongst children working together or, it is argued, from a computer-based learning programme. You can read more about this in Pollard (1996, Section 6.4).

Example: *A teacher is working with the whole class during the daily mathematics lesson. She revises the work the children have covered to this point. She asks them to think of another way of tackling the problem they have been working on. With careful questions and prompts she guides them towards an understanding of an alternative approach.*

Vygotsky and Bruner emphasise the importance of the social and cultural context in which learning takes place. Learning is seen not solely as the work of the individual learner but as a social process. Applied to the classroom, it is the theory which underpins group and collaborative approaches such as those of investigative work in science or technology, shared writing or problem solving.

Example: *A group of three children are drafting a letter to invite members of the local pensioners' club to their class assembly. They discuss the factual content of the letter, how it should be addressed and what would make it appealing to the elderly people they are inviting. One of them reads the draft to the rest of the class, inviting comments or suggestions for improvement. A second draft is written based on these comments and when they are happy with this, a final copy is produced ready for posting.*

Bruner's work (1986) has continued to develop the social constructivist view, which has strongly influenced the curriculum and teaching approaches in British schools since the 1970s. Emphasising the social context of learning, he sees the child as an active processor of information. The cultural context in which learning takes place is important. Learning becomes a process of making sense of and extending the child's understanding, which is derived from his or her culture.

In the classroom, Bruner's work is associated with the notion of a spiral curriculum, in which topics are revisited, over time, in order to develop a more mature understanding. This corresponds to Bruner's theory of a three-stage process of learning:

➲ enactive – the child learns by doing (rather as in Piaget's first two stages); this stage relies on the use of objects and physical models in learning and the child's understanding is shown by the way in which he or she manipulates these materials and models;
➲ iconic – at this stage pictures and drawings support the child's learning and record or represent the enactive stage; the child communicates understanding using pictures;
➲ symbolic – the child is able to learn in an abstract medium and use symbols and signs including writing to explain the iconic or enactive elements.

Example: *In Year 1, Lauren learns coin values playing in the class shop. In Year 2, she returns to learning about money doing simple calculations with coins. In Key Stage 2 she is able to work on calculations and problems expressed only in words, numbers and symbols.*

Example: *Sam, in reception, plays with a set of shapes, sorting them by shape and colour. In Year 2, he is given a right-angled piece of card and has to find items in the classroom which have right angles, matching these with the card. In Year 4 Sam is able to measure 90-degree angles using a protractor.*

Although these examples illustrate different levels in Bruner's three-stage process of learning, in reality a child may move backwards and forwards between them.

National Curriculum, National Literacy and Numeracy Strategies

Social constructivist thinking has influenced the development of the National Curriculum. The National Curriculum was introduced in 1988 and revised in 1995, following considerable criticism from teachers and others due to the overloaded curriculum it imposed. Further revision led to the publication of Curriculum 2000. As well as the detailed requirements for each subject, the National Curriculum identifies cross-curricular issues as well as key skills and thinking skills which children should acquire. The cross-curricular issues encompass spiritual, moral, health, social and cultural education, citizenship, inclusion, language across the curriculum, the use of ICT, and health and safety matters. The key skills identified are those of communication, application of number, information technology, working with others, improving one's own learning and performance, and problem solving. The National Curriculum also outlines a range of thinking skills which complement these key skills.

Towards the end of the 1990s the National Literacy Strategy and National Numeracy Strategy were also introduced into schools. These frameworks set out a detailed and structured approach to teaching literacy and numeracy based on a daily lesson in each subject. The strategies applied to schools in England and although not statutory, they have been adopted by most schools, sometimes in an adapted form. Many schools in Wales also use these strategies.

Evidence from international comparisons of attainment was influential in the curriculum developments of the 1990s. The National Numeracy Strategy, in particular, was a response to evidence from international comparisons made during the mid-1990s which measured the attainment of upper primary and lower secondary age children in more than 50 countries. This showed that British school children performed relatively well in some areas of mathematics, such as data handling and shape and space, compared with their peers in other countries. However, in most aspects, including numeracy, they achieved well below the standard of children in many other countries. Some countries, such as Korea, Japan, Singapore and Hungary, did exceptionally well in comparison with the rest. This prompted research into the success of the teaching methods in these countries, particularly Hungary, and it is this research that underpins the National Numeracy Strategy.

Howard Gardner and multiple intelligences

The work of Howard Gardner (1993), and the proposal that there are a number of different types of intelligence, has also had considerable influence on our understanding of learning over the past decade or so. Gardner rejects the traditional view of intelligence, particularly two assumptions: that it is a single, general capacity that the individual possesses to a greater or lesser extent, and that it can be measured with relatively simple tests. Gardner proposes that there are a number of human intelligences and that the fostering and development of all these capacities should be the concern of the teacher. It is also a factor to be borne in mind when devising learning activities for children or grouping them to work on a collaborative task. Gardner's multiple intelligences are outlined briefly below.

Linguistic	a capacity with language and patterns and a desire to explore them
Mathematical and logical	a learner who succeeds at abstract, logical and structured thinking, discerning their relationships and underlying principles
Visual and spatial	this intelligence relates to a facility with pictures and mental images, diagrams and graphical representation; the visual and spatial learner has a capacity to perceive the visual world accurately and will be able to transform and modify their perceptions
Musical	not only a capacity in composing and performing but also an ability to respond to mood and emotion, rhythm, timbre and structure in music
Interpersonal	the capacity to establish good relationships with others, to discern mood, feelings and mental state in others and to communicate effectively
Intra-personal	the capacity for self-awareness and self-knowledge and the ability to discern one's own emotions
Kinaesthetic	the ability to use the body and objects in highly differentiated and skilled ways; the person with kinaesthetic intelligence likes to make and touch whilst learning

Since he first put forward these ideas, Gardner has added an eighth category to his analysis, that of naturalist intelligence, which he describes as the facility to recognise and categorise natural objects.

Gardner claims that all human beings possess all these capacities. In practice, each individual will have his or her own profile, reflecting differing levels of ability in the different intelligences. In terms of the classroom, you need to think about the range of learning experiences you offer children. Do these experiences reflect the range of capacities you are likely to find across the class, or are they narrowly focused, likely to lead to success only for children with linguistic or mathematical ability?

Example: *The class is studying characterisation in English. Rather than asking them to describe in writing the characters in a narrative, the teacher invites them to represent the character through the use of role play, oil pastels, dance, or by composing sound pictures of the characters using tuned and untuned percussion instruments.*

Planning a range of different types of activities will give the children in your class the best possible opportunity to achieve success.

You are now ready to complete the needs analysis linked to this theme in order to know how you might best proceed with your learning.

Assessment

How far have you developed your understanding of how children learn and teachers teach? Reflect on the needs analysis table below and if possible discuss your ideas and your evidence with a colleague, teacher or tutor.

Getting Started	Date/ evidence	Developing your Skills	Date/ evidence	Extending your Skills	Date/ evidence
		I have read the teaching and learning policy and discussed this with my teacher.			
I have observed teaching in the classroom.				I have observed different types of questioning.	
I can identify the theoretical basis for the teaching approaches being used.				I can identify the types of questions being used, their purposes and effect.	
		I have observed children and listed the opportunities for structured play or exploration.		I have observed the children's responses to the teacher's questions.	
		I can plan and teach activities, taking account of different theories of learning.		I can plan activities that reflect a variety of learning styles.	
				I can plan and use a range of different questions when teaching.	
I can reflect on the appropriateness of particular teaching approaches used across different subjects.		I can evaluate the children's learning and use this information to reflect on the suitability of the teaching approach I used.		I can evaluate the effectiveness of my questioning skills.	
				I am able to review whether the activities I planned took account of children's different learning styles.	
*If one or more of these is not yet ticked, you may find it helpful to complete the activities on **pages 47–49**.*		*If one or more of these is not yet ticked, you may find it helpful to complete the activities on **pages 71–75**.*		*If one or more of these is not yet ticked, you may find it helpful to complete the activities on **pages 103–106**.*	

Chapter 2   How do you create a learning environment?

This section explores the importance of the learning environment and the ways in which it can contribute to children's well-being and enhance their learning. Many of the influences which affect the learning environment are outlined. In this section you will be exploring:

- the nature of the learning environment;
- the context within which it is created and managed;
- the aims of the teacher which the learning environment can be used to support.

What is the learning environment?

This theme explores the ways in which the teacher can enhance children's learning through sensitive and practical management of the learning environment. The term 'learning environment' has been chosen rather than classroom to emphasise that there are wider issues here. It is not just the organisation of people and furniture in a room, although these are important aspects which will be covered. The learning environment includes three elements which are outlined below.

Ethos
Confident children generally feel secure in their environment and are better able to learn and make good progress. Shared behavioural and learning goals help children to develop independence and self-discipline through responsibility and high expectations. The use of positive reinforcement, rather than punishments or sanctions, should work alongside this. Children need opportunities to explore, investigate and discuss as part of the learning process and should be encouraged to take risks in their learning, not always searching for the one 'right' answer. Each member of the class has something to contribute – their ability to do so will depend on their personal relationships with the teacher and each other.

Organisation
The timetable lays out the order and length of lessons and should be made clear to children so that they have a sense of what each day and each lesson holds for them. Children will feel safe and secure if useful routines are established to make lessons run smoothly and efficiently. Children will need to be grouped in different ways to suit each lesson. Lesson content may be suited to whole class work, to group or paired collaboration or to individual work.

Physical environment
This may be inside or outside the classroom and includes areas such as the tables where the children sit, the reading corner, cloakrooms, entrance hall, the class and/ or school library. In addition, the physical environment will include shared areas of the school such as the hall, playground, sports field, garden and conservation area and even local facilities and destinations for educational visits. The resources available to the teacher and children, such as furniture, displays and other adults, will all be part of the physical environment which has to be managed.

Context

As a teacher, you are responsible for organising the children and classroom. There are many influences which will affect your decisions. These are not necessarily limiting factors but can provide new challenges and opportunities for teachers and schools.

Legal and political

The National Curriculum is a statutory document which lays out the subjects and content you are required to teach. This will affect the way in which you organise and manage the learning environment.

Example: *The fact that you are required to teach practical subjects such as art and design and technology means that you will need more space and equipment than if the curriculum included only formal teaching of reading and writing.*

Other non-statutory but influential documents include the National Literacy Strategy (NLS), the National Numeracy Strategy (NNS) and the Curriculum Guidance for the Foundation Stage. These imply methods of teaching and organisation as well as content.

Example: *Both the NLS and NNS contain lesson structures which include whole class, group and individual work, requiring spaces and resources conducive to these styles of working.*

LEA

Your Local Education Authority will be concerned with raising standards in all its schools and will therefore have its own priorities relating to inspections from OFSTED and national comparative statistics. These will be clearly communicated through advisory staff and head teachers. It may be that a particular curriculum area, or a wider issue such as parental involvement or local community relations, is a priority. In any case, this will filter through to individual teachers and may require them to organise children, classrooms and resources in particular ways.

Example: *In response to an LEA initiative to encourage parental involvement in schools, the school puts up a noticeboard to display curriculum plans and other important information.*

Parents and the local community

The school is a central point of any community, whether it is rural, suburban or inner-city. The influences of local people and groups will therefore be strongly felt and should be carefully channelled and used as a positive factor rather than one causing conflict. Parents and local communities will have aspirations and expectations which are influenced by their socio-economic, cultural and religious backgrounds. These will affect the school as a whole as well as individual classes and teachers.

Example: *There may be a need for extra teaching and support for children with English as an additional language and this will affect the use of learning support assistants and teachers throughout the school. It may also affect the wider curriculum, teaching and learning strategies adopted and timetabling.*

Example: *In some areas, where there is a high number of families in which both parents work, it may be necessary and prudent to provide breakfast clubs and after-school care. This may involve the organisation of extra activities and staff as well as the possible use of classrooms and facilities outside normal school hours.*

School

The school itself, its teachers, head teacher, governors, support staff, ethos and policies will be the influence felt most keenly by class teachers. The ethos and atmosphere of a school is determined largely by the governors, head teacher and the relationships between staff. These relationships will affect the shared view of the roles and responsibilities of teachers and policy decisions such as display, handwriting and the use of shared resources.

Example: The decision to group children into sets for particular subjects (frequently English and mathematics) will have considerable consequences for teachers. This could involve the organisation of children from other classes, their movement around the school and the need for suitable resources to be available concurrently in more than one classroom. There are also issues of self-esteem and avoidance of labelling children, possibly having a negative effect on their learning and personal development.

Buildings

Schools can vary enormously in their age, location and design, all of which provide opportunities and challenges for teachers. The size and shape of the classroom and its position in relation to other classrooms are variables which are difficult to alter. Other features such as the position of carpeted areas, furniture and resources can be more easily changed or worked around and should be used to best effect by the teacher.

Example: A Victorian school building may have high windows, thick walls and damp patches. It may also have well-proportioned classrooms with plenty of display space and large storage cupboards, wide corridors and an assembly hall. A school built in the 1960s may have large open-plan teaching areas, other versatile workspaces, large windows and purpose-built office and staffroom areas. It may, however, be lacking in accessible display areas, appropriate storage and quiet spaces for whole class work and more formal teaching styles.

Every type of school building will affect the organisation of the classes within it. Each will provide opportunities as well as difficulties to overcome. The challenge for the teacher is to transform this into a stimulating learning environment for children and a functional working environment for adults. This is possible through careful and creative use of the resources available and should reflect the classroom ethos.

Example: If you wish to encourage children to take some responsibility for their learning and develop independence and self-discipline, they must have access to resources which enable them to do this. Shutting everything away in cupboards will make the classroom tidier but will not allow children to make choices about what they need or what approach they find most effective for a particular piece of work. Labelling resources, drawers and shelves clearly will enable children to find what they need and take responsibility for looking after it and replacing it when the work is completed.

Children

Each child is an individual and will have personal needs which must be met if they are to become a successful learner. The learning environment will need to be reviewed constantly and altered in order to meet children's needs and to be positive and stimulating for all. For example, some children may not speak English as their first language, others may have specific special educational needs such as a visual impairment or dyslexia. All children will differ in more subtle ways such as their preferred learning style, level of independence or social development. Each class of children will vary in terms of their capabilities, social dynamics and emotional needs.

Example: Younger children, or those with English as an additional language, may find it difficult to read labels. Symbols, colours, pictures or photographs can be used as well as the words. This will enable children to find what they need and reinforce word recognition. Similarly, visually impaired children may need labels to be available in Braille to allow them to work more independently.

Example: A display relating to a current science topic should include apparatus to encourage hands-on investigation as well as posters and books containing text and images. This will appeal to children with different learning styles.

Teacher

The children's learning environment is also the teacher's working environment and must meet the needs of both. Of course, the needs of the teacher are closely linked to the needs of the children and the smooth operation of the learning environment will occur when each complements the other. Teachers have different styles of teaching and this may change from one lesson to the next or even within one lesson, to suit the content and needs of the children. Teachers work with other adults in the classroom – learning support assistants and parent helpers – and sometimes team teach, collaborating with other teachers in order to provide the widest range of learning experiences for the children.

Aims

Wherever you teach and whatever age group you are teaching, there are some common aims which you will share with your colleagues.

Children should be:	*The environment should be:*
Happy and confident	Secure and shared by all
Enthusiastic	Encouraging
Independent learners	Stimulating
Creative thinkers	Well organised and maintained
Skilful and knowledgeable	Equipped with appropriate and attractive resources
Offered purposeful activities	

There is no simple answer as to how to achieve this, but the important thing to remember is that it will not happen unless the teacher creates an environment in which this is possible. Creating a learning environment in which all children feel safe, secure and stimulated is challenging and undoubtedly relies upon the teacher keeping all these elements in mind when making careful decisions about the organisation of the children, classroom and resources. The keys to success are:

➲ flexibility;
➲ responsiveness;
➲ communication;
➲ organisation.

You are now ready to complete the needs analysis linked to this theme in order to know how you might best proceed with your learning.

Assessment

How far have you developed your understanding of creating a learning environment? Reflect on the needs analysis table below and if possible discuss your ideas and your evidence with a colleague, teacher or tutor.

Getting Started	Date/ evidence	Developing your Skills	Date/ evidence	Extending your Skills	Date/ evidence
I am aware of the necessity for clear rules and routines in the classroom.		When working with the whole class I can use a range of strategies to ensure that transition periods are smooth and do not disrupt learning.		I am aware of the whole school policy for behaviour management and can use it consistently.	
As a result of teaching individuals and small groups I can identify which rules and routines have worked best for me.					
When teaching a group of children I can use established routines effectively.		I can stop the class and gain attention when necessary.			
I have observed the ways in which teachers make their expectations for behaviour explicit and reinforce these.		I have observed how a teacher communicates different expectations to individual children within the class.			
When teaching a group of children I can make clear expectations for behaviour and use positive feedback to communicate when these have been achieved.		When teaching groups and the whole class I can differentiate and communicate clearly my expectations for behaviour and learning.		I am able to use a range of strategies to agree and implement appropriate expectations for behaviour.	
I have observed and recognise the need for lessons to be broken down into carefully timed sections.		I have developed a range of purposeful activities that can be used for short interactions with the class.		I can plan to ensure a variety of learning opportunities within the structure of the class timetable, negotiating minor changes where appropriate.	
I have observed how children access, use and take responsibility for resources.		I have completed a resource audit.			
		When planning for the whole class I can identify and organise the required resources well in advance.			
I understand the need to organise classroom resources in different ways according to the needs of the learners.		I have observed and understand the importance of managing children, resources and activities, but recognise that this can be achieved in a variety of ways.		I can anticipate potential dangers and difficulties and use information from the school's health and safety policy to adjust my teaching accordingly.	
		I recognise and can use a variety of groupings according to the purpose and focus of the lesson.			
		I can plan for effective use of other adults in the classroom to ensure successful learning and assessment of children's progress.		I can communicate with other adults in the classroom, providing them with plans and making use of their feedback for assessment purposes.	
*If one or more of these is not yet ticked, you may find it helpful to complete the activities on **pages 50–52**.*		*If one or more of these is not yet ticked, you may find it helpful to complete the activities on **pages 76–81**.*		*If one or more of these is not yet ticked, you may find it helpful to complete the activities on **pages 107–111**.*	

Chapter 2   How do you plan for learning and teaching?

This section will help you understand the various elements of curriculum planning, from whole school long-term planning, medium-term and weekly planning to the planning of individual lessons. As a trainee you will need to understand the importance of each of these types and be able to plan effectively both for children's learning and for your professional development. The statutory basis of curriculum planning will be explored and the various documents that will inform your planning will be discussed. This section will cover:

➲ why plan?
➲ types of planning;
➲ policies and schemes of work;
➲ what is the statutory basis for planning?
➲ so how do teachers actually plan?

Why plan?

When you first visit a well-managed primary classroom you could be misled into thinking that the teaching and learning you see is something that 'just happens'. Nothing could be further from the truth. The smooth organisation is based on the sort of detailed attention to classroom organisation discussed in the previous section. You will probably see the teacher relating to the children with ease, communicating, managing, inspiring and encouraging individuals or groups. But teaching that may appear effortless and natural is based on a great deal of detailed planning. Teachers in primary schools spend a considerable proportion of their working week planning for their teaching in the classroom. As a newcomer to the profession you will probably have to spend even longer on planning than do the experienced colleagues working alongside you.

Knowing that your lessons are carefully planned will help give you confidence in the classroom. Planning is important not just because it contributes to the smooth running of activities in the classroom but also because of a shared responsibility and accountability for the work of the school as a whole. Planning may be monitored by other people such as the head teacher, or by individual subject leaders who share the responsibility for the quality of teaching in particular subjects throughout the school. In a teacher's absence, written planning enables a colleague or supply teacher to take over the class and carry on teaching them, providing maximum continuity for children's learning.

In most schools, planning is both a collaborative and an individual process. You may find that you will meet each week with colleagues, both teachers and support staff, to undertake some shared planning and then work alone on planning the detail of your own teaching.

Types of planning

Generally, teachers will undertake several types of planning, often referred to as long-, medium- and short-term planning, as well as specific plans for each lesson.

Long-term planning will usually have been completed by staff as a whole, sharing out the material to be taught throughout one or more key stages so as to provide adequate coverage of the curriculum. Teachers will have negotiated between them which aspects of the curriculum will be covered in each year group.

The purpose of medium-term planning is to provide greater detail and ensure that there is continuity and progression in teaching. The term 'medium-term planning' may be used slightly differently in individual schools, but is generally understood to be the work to be covered over a period of half a term to a term. Sometimes this may be referred to as a unit of work. It is at the level of medium-term planning that you can focus on the common aspects of a number of subjects so that children are able to learn in a context that is meaningful to them. This will help them make links between different aspects of their learning. Often, much of the material to be taught will be drawn together under a topic title which gives coherence to the curriculum as it is received by the children. It may be that not all of the content to be taught fits easily within that topic, in which case it may be preferable to teach some aspects of the work discretely rather than make tenuous links to the main topic. Some topics may have a dominant theme or subject, such as a history or science-led topic; some subjects may be omitted entirely.

Example: *A teacher plans a topic called 'Legions of the Eagle' for her Year 4 class. Within this topic heading she aims to cover aspects of the National Curriculum in history, geography, music, art and design technology. Work that the children have been doing in their daily literacy lessons will be reinforced by a range of activities including writing eyewitness accounts of a battle between the Romans and the Celts. In Year 4 they have to cover some aspects of electricity in science, and as this does not fit into the topic it will be covered through a separate mini-project. Below is an overview showing how some of these subjects have been linked in the planning.*

	English	Mathematics	History	Music	Design and technology	Art and design
Week one	Explore the vocabulary associated with an army marching.	Compare different number systems including Roman numerals and the use of 0 in place value.	Who were the Romans? Who were the Celts? When, why and how did they invade Britain?	Explore the sounds of an army; research instruments from around the world and from the past.	Explore properties of clay.	Research Roman mosaics.
Week two	Explore the vocabulary associated with battles.	Explore the Repeat command in Logo.	Time line activities.	Explore the rhythm of an army marching.	Make clay tiles using impressed and applied decoration.	
Week three	Poetry based on battle sounds.	Create simple procedures in Logo.	Caesar's account of the invasion in 55BC and hot seat activity.	Recreate 'army' using tuned and untuned percussion, body percussion and vocal sounds – focus on rhythm and dynamics.	Make clay tiles using impressed and applied decoration.	Research Celtic patterns.
Week four	News flashes from the battle aimed at different audiences.	Use Repeat command and/or simple procedures in Logo to produce Celtic patterns.	Celtic resistance and co-operation.	Recreate 'army' using tuned and untuned percussion, body percussion and vocal sounds – focus on tempo.	Design mosaic.	Use a range of printing techniques to produce Celtic patterns.
Week five	Newspaper reports of battle from perspective of Romans or Celts.	Use Repeat command and/or simple procedures in Logo to produce Celtic patterns.	Celtic and Roman perceptions of the battle.	Compose sound picture of Roman and Celtic battle.	Plan mosaic using squared paper. Evaluate plans and select one to make.	Use a range of printing techniques to produce Celtic patterns.
Week six	Performance based on poetry, newsflashes and music.			Performance based on poetry, newsflashes and music.	Make class mosaic using terrazzo.	

This is not all the teaching that is going on in this class, it simply shows the links that can be made between subjects to provide a meaningful context for children's learning. The work in the literacy hour and the daily mathematics lesson is unlikely to fit easily into this plan, although there may be opportunities for children to apply their skills and understanding in maths and English to tasks which form part of the topic work. It is important not to make tenuous links when planning. Work which does not fit into the plan should be taught discretely.

When you plan in this way you can ensure that there is progression within each subject and coherence across the week. For example, in week three the children will research Celtic patterns, which are geometric, whilst exploring the use of simple procedures in Logo to make geometric patterns. They will be writing poetry based on a battle theme and also exploring the use of rhythm and dynamics to produce music representing the Roman and Celtic armies.

You can see that there is also progression through the weeks in different subjects, enabling children to consolidate and develop their skills and understanding. In music, for example, the children will begin by discussing the sounds associated with an army and researching instruments of the past and from different parts of the world. The next week they will explore the rhythms of an army marching. In weeks three and four they will develop the theme of 'army', focusing first on rhythm and dynamics and then on tempo. The following week they will use this new understanding to compose a sound picture representing a battle between the Romans and the Celts. In week six they will bring this together with their work in English to create a performance.

Involving parents

Schools often display copies of the medium-term planning in the class for parents to see or send copies of it home with the children. This ensures that parents are informed about what their children will be learning. It also means that parents can contribute to the work of the class. They may have books or resources they would be willing to lend or expertise they could share with the children.

Short-term planning

Short-term planning generally refers to a weekly breakdown of what you are going to teach. This will usually be set out in the form of a table, showing the subjects to be covered and giving brief details of the content of teaching and planned activities. From the information on the weekly plan you will produce a plan for each individual lesson you teach, which will provide greater detail about the content, organisation and activities in your lesson.

Often, plans for the literacy hour and the daily mathematics lesson are completed in greater detail than the planning in other subjects. Weekly planning in literacy and numeracy may cover more than one unit of work and extend over a period of several weeks. Most schools adopt detailed weekly planning in these subjects as well as planning for the medium and long-term. In addition to this, you may work to a timetable which sets out the organisation of the school week on a day-by-day basis. This is discussed in more detail on **pages 107–108**.

When you begin your work in school you will probably find that long and medium-term planning is already in place, but you will have to complete short-term and individual lesson plans for each lesson you teach.

Policies and schemes of work

All the planning undertaken in the school should reflect the philosophy and teaching approaches expressed in its own curriculum policies and schemes of work. A curriculum policy is a document setting out the principles which underpin the teaching of a particular subject. It is likely to express the school's view about the nature of the subject itself, why it is of value, and the aims and objectives which relate to the teaching of that subject. It may also have other statements relating to teaching approaches, special educational needs (SEN) in that subject, inclusion, English as an additional language and so on. A scheme of work sets out in greater detail the content of what is to be taught in each subject and the teaching strategies to be adopted, usually on a year-by-year basis.

What is the statutory basis for planning?

In England and Wales the National Curriculum is the statutory basis for what is taught in schools in Key Stages 1 to 4, the period of compulsory schooling from five to sixteen. The National Curriculum for the primary stage recognises three core subjects. These are English, mathematics and science. The remaining seven are referred to as foundation subjects. These are information and communications technology, history, geography, art and design, music, design and technology and physical education. There are some differences between the National Curricula of England and Wales, including the fact that in Wales, Welsh is a compulsory subject of the National Curriculum. Although the National Curriculum determines the content in terms of the knowledge, skills and understanding to be taught, teaching methods are not prescribed. It is up to each school to determine its teaching approaches and these are usually expressed in its curriculum policies.

Religious education is not part of the National Curriculum, although it must be taught in schools. The content of the RE curriculum for state schools is determined locally in each Local Education Authority by a Standing Committee on Religious Education which includes representatives from major faith groups. Parents have the right to withdraw their children from religious education (and from the daily act of worship) if they wish. In voluntary-aided or church schools the RE curriculum may be based on documents produced by the particular faith group concerned and reflect the beliefs of that denomination.

In the foundation stage, which covers children from three to five, planning is generally based on the areas of learning outlined in the Curriculum Guidance for the Foundation Stage, published by the Qualifications and Curriculum Agency (QCA). This is the document which gives guidance on the curriculum for the under-fives in various settings. The curriculum is expressed in terms of six areas of learning:

- personal, social and emotional development;
- communication, language and literacy;
- mathematical development;
- knowledge and understanding of the world;
- physical development;
- creative development.

Although the National Curriculum sets out the legal requirements, there are a number of other documents used by teachers to support and inform curriculum planning. The National Literacy and Numeracy Strategies are used for planning daily literacy and mathematics lessons and whilst not a statutory requirement, most schools work from these documents. The QCA has produced Schemes of Work and these are also used extensively in schools as the basis of planning for the foundation subjects of the curriculum.

Many schools do not rely solely on QCA documentation but use other sources such as schemes of work produced by their Local Education Authority or by commercial publishers. Schools often produce their own schemes of work, based on the requirements of the National Curriculum, which may draw on materials from a number of sources such as those already mentioned.

So how do teachers actually plan?

Teachers will usually meet at the start of a block of time such as a half term or term and plan what is to be taught in each year group over the coming weeks. In larger schools, there may be more than one class and the staff will usually plan the work collaboratively. In smaller schools, there may be only one teacher in each year, or even a single class covering two or more year groups. Even where there is only one teacher covering a year group, planning is often undertaken collaboratively, as there may be other support staff who contribute to the process. Often staff from two or more year groups meet to plan together, to ensure continuity and benefit from an exchange of ideas and sharing of expertise.

You are now ready to complete the needs analysis linked to this theme in order to know how you might best proceed with your learning.

Assessment

How far have you developed your understanding of how to plan for learning and teaching? Reflect on the needs analysis table below and if possible discuss your ideas and your evidence with a colleague, teacher or tutor.

Getting Started	Date/evidence	Developing your Skills	Date/evidence	Extending your Skills	Date/evidence
I have read curriculum policies for all the subjects I am going to teach and discussed these with my teacher.		I have read the NLS and NNS medium-term plans for my class and discussed these with my teacher.		I have read the long-term planning and the relevant schemes of work for the class I am teaching.	
I have evaluated the teacher's planning and I understand its purpose and content.					
I can plan a lesson for a group using clear learning objectives and base this on the teacher's planning.		I have planned a sequence of lessons including science and some other foundation subjects. I have written an overview grid for these subjects.		I have produced a medium-term plan and discussed this with my teacher.	
		I can produce weekly plans based on the NLS and NNS.			
I can evaluate my lessons in terms of the children's learning and my own learning.		I can evaluate and amend my planning after teaching on a daily and weekly basis.		I can review my medium-term planning and reflect on the process of planning.	
*If one or more of these is not yet ticked, you may find it helpful to complete the activities on **pages 53–57**.*		*If one or more of these is not yet ticked, you may find it helpful to complete the activities on **pages 82–84**.*		*If one or more of these is not yet ticked, you may find it helpful to complete the activities on **pages 112–114**.*	

Chapter 2 — How do you assess and record children's learning?

This section will help you to consider the role of assessment and how this can affect teaching and learning. It is important to understand the variety of assessment strategies that can be used to gather evidence on children's learning and attainment. These have different purposes and audiences. As a trainee you will need to make decisions about how you carry out assessment in the classroom and use the information gathered from this to inform your teaching and promote learning. This section will cover:

➲ what do we mean by assessment?
➲ why assess?
➲ background on changes and developments of the national assessment framework;
➲ what are the potential difficulties, problems or challenges of assessment?
➲ how can we ensure that our assessment is directed towards promoting learning?

What do we mean by assessment?

Assessment should be an integral part of the learning and teaching process. The term 'assessment' refers to all those activities undertaken by teachers which provide information to be used as feedback to modify the teaching and learning activities in which they are engaged (Black and Wiliam 1998, page 2).

A major review of research on classroom assessment and its impact was carried out by Black and Wiliam (1998) and summarised within the pamphlet *Inside the Black Box*. This review confirmed that if carried out effectively, informal classroom assessment with constructive feedback to children will raise levels of attainment.

Why assess?

The Assessment Reform Group (1999, page 2) has stated that:

> '...assessment which is explicitly designed to promote learning is the single most powerful tool we have for both raising standards and empowering lifelong learners.'

This builds on the findings of Black and Wiliam (1998) in their review of the research and the authors are confident in their conclusion that the quality of children's learning can be enhanced by improving formative assessment and feedback, although they recognise the complexity of this challenge. Assessment should also take account of both *what* and *how* children learn. In this way the teacher can focus on the curriculum content covered by the child and their understanding of this, but also evaluate how the child is learning and whether any adaptations need to be made to the teaching strategies or methods being used. All assessments should help teachers to plan more effectively. Teachers need to use their assessment information to modify either the curriculum offered, their own practice, the teaching approaches used or a combination of any of these. It is also important to note children's attitudes to learning as these can provide valuable information about their motivation, self-esteem or even how they view themselves 'as a learner'.

Background on changes and developments of the national assessment framework

Before looking at the practical issues related to assessment in all its varied guises it is important to gain some understanding of the background context and development of assessment over the past 15 years or so.

A national framework for assessment and testing was first introduced into England with the implementation of the 1988 Education Reform Act and the arrival of the National Curriculum. At this point a Task Group for Assessment and Testing (TGAT) was convened to identify the nature and content of this national framework and to offer suggestions to the government and teachers as to how it should be implemented. TGAT identified four criteria for this assessment system. It recommended that it should be 'criterion-referenced' and thus related to what the children can do. It should be 'formative' and so provide a foundation for a teacher to make appropriate decisions about future learning needs for individuals and groups. In order for judgements to be consistent and fair across schools it needed to be 'moderated'. Finally, it suggested that it must 'relate to progression' and so reflect anticipated routes of children's development and learning. However, what was set up in schools generally took the form of two very different types of assessment, each with a very different purpose. These are referred to as summative and formative assessment.

Summative and formative assessment

These assessment procedures enabled schools to keep parents informed about their children's progress as well as providing a means of comparing schools. This kind of assessment measures the result of learning and can be viewed as 'assessment of learning'. It is called summative assessment and now occurs in classrooms at the end of a phase/period of learning (such as at the end of a topic or term) or at a particular time such as in the case of Statutory Assessment Tasks (SATs). Baseline assessments completed for children in the autumn term in which they start school are another form of summative assessment. However, the results of these baseline assessments should also be used formatively to inform future work with individual children. It has been suggested by Lindsay (1998) that the purposes of baseline assessment fall into two distinct categories. The first has a focus on the child and would therefore result from the formative assessment function identified above. In other words, how can this child's learning and developmental needs best be met? The second category has a focus on the school. It is this summative purpose that is increasingly being used in schools to predict a child's progress by making comparisons with national data and thus indicate the potential or expected achievement of this child when they take the end of Key Stage 1 SATs two-and-a-half years later.

The second very different type of assessment is that of formative assessment or 'assessment for learning'. This is based on a teacher's recognition that continuous assessment of children is an invaluable source of information to inform future planning. If teachers gather evidence of children's responses, they can shape and alter their teaching to best meet their needs. This kind of assessment for learning is appropriate in all situations and helps to identify the next steps in order to build on success or strengths as well as to correct or support weaknesses. This kind of assessment should occur all the time in classrooms and is evident in the national assessment framework through 'teacher assessment'.

Example: *If Billy (aged nine) has demonstrated that he can already recognise, name and describe the properties of different triangles, then when the rest of the class continue working on this the next day, he will clearly need more challenging work. Perhaps his teacher could ask him to create as many different types of triangles as possible using elastic bands on a geoboard (pin board).*

Following the Dearing Review (1993) of the National Curriculum and the assessment procedures, a new National Curriculum and revised assessment procedures were implemented in September 1995. The term 'attainment target' was redefined in the revised Curriculum 2000 document. In this it is used to describe the 'knowledge, skills and understanding that pupils of different abilities and maturities are expected to have by the end of each Key Stage' (Curriculum 2000, page 1 of attainment targets section). For Key Stages 1 and 2 each attainment target is made up of six level descriptions. Each level description describes the types and range of performance that children working at that level should characteristically demonstrate. These should be used by teachers to determine the attainment level of each of their children at the end of each Key Stage as well as in the SATs. The following statement about the status and relationship between teacher assessment and end of Key Stage assessment tasks was made:

> 'Teacher assessment is an essential part of the National Curriculum assessment and reporting arrangements. Both have equal status and provide complementary information about children's attainment. The tests provide a "snapshot" of attainment at the end of the Key Stage, while teacher assessment, carried out as part of teaching and learning in the classroom, covers the full range and scope of the programmes of study, and takes account of the evidence of achievements in a range of contexts, including that gained through discussion and observation.'
> (SCAA 1997, KS 1 & 2 Assessment Arrangements)

This confirms that the ongoing judgements made by teachers are of considerable value and add to the range of evidence that is available on children's leaning. The tests (SATs) themselves do not 'tell the full story'.

Now that you are familiar with some of the changes and developments in the national assessment framework since its introduction in 1988 we will go on to look in more detail at some of the key issues regarding the process of assessment, the selection and use of different strategies to carry out assessment of children's learning.

What are the potential difficulties, problems or challenges of assessment?

Validity versus reliability

One of the key difficulties concerns the relationship between validity and reliability. Valid assessment methods are those that assess what they are claiming to assess. Validity of assessment can be improved by drawing on a range of information about a child's attainment and progress and using a number of assessment techniques. However, this adds to the complexity of the task and may render the process unmanageable. For those teachers working in early years settings there are also concerns regarding when it is appropriate to make outcome judgements of this kind about a child and when this could be seen as simply indicative of their developmental level and pathway, which may be very different to that of their peers.

Reliability is linked to consistency. Procedures need to be implemented in ways which ensure consistency in the assessments between different teachers and school settings and from year to year to allow comparisons to be made. If the reliability is low, judgements must be seen as inconsistent, unfair and unreliable. To increase reliability one needs to simplify the procedures and focus, which tends to result in tests, particularly pencil and paper ones.

Example: *It is hard, if not impossible, to devise a pencil and paper test which can be used to easily assess a child's curiosity or creativity even though these are important features of their development and learning and therefore aspects in which we might be interested as teachers. In contrast, it is relatively easy to devise a written question which assesses the skill of reading a thermometer accurately, or even whether a child can apply this knowledge and select an appropriate scale for a thermometer which is going to be used to test the temperature at which water boils.*

The tension between these two aspects of validity and reliability is evident in the changes and modifications to the national assessment procedures since their instigation in 1988. For further reading refer to Gipps and Stobart (1993) as well as Gipps C (1994).

The drive to ensure reliability and consistency has led to some schools developing portfolios containing samples of work in different curriculum areas which have been agreed by the staff to represent each attainment target level description within the National Curriculum. Head teachers may use staff meetings to engage staff in the process of levelling work to ensure that all members of the team can make accurate judgements and level across the primary range of attainment, regardless of which particular year group individuals are teaching at the time.

Relationships

There is a danger that the pressure exerted on teachers to produce good results through the performance of their children could impact on the relationship between the teacher and the children or between the children themselves. The right ethos needs to be created so that respect and trust are shared by all those working together in the classroom. In this way children will take risks in their learning and admit when they are stuck or confused. Children should be aware of their own learning and where they need to go next, and be actively involved in the assessment process. If this is carried out effectively, children should not be anxious or worried about 'letting themselves or the teacher down'. However, it is possible that the tendency for teachers to teach 'to the test' and even practise test papers in KS2 could have an extremely detrimental effect on some children's learning and self-esteem. It is common practice now for most schools to use the optional SATs papers in Years 3, 4 and 5 whilst the Year 2 and 6 children are taking their end of Key Stage statutory assessments. This summative assessment (or assessment of learning) may not support successful learning or promote assessment for learning.

There is also a danger that children see assessment as a tool which labels them and a source of anxiety, rather than something which enables them to become more successful learners. This is likely to seriously affect the low-attaining children in a class, for whom school can easily be linked to a daily sense of failure. Alongside this issue, consider the messages we convey to children through the increasing use of setting, streaming and attainment groups as an organisational and management tool. Children are extremely perceptive even at a very young age and often know exactly who is in which group and why. This can be another source of concern and anxiety for children. If assessment is genuinely used to monitor progress and inform future teaching, we must consider the role of such attainment groupings and how often these are reviewed.

Example: *Susannah has rather weak numerical and calculating skills and so is in the low-attaining mathematics group. She sees herself as a 'poor mathematician' even though she has excellent spatial awareness skills and understanding in this strand of mathematics equivalent to that of the high-attaining group. However, the teacher does not move her into a different group for a unit of work on shape and space. Why not? What impact could the good use of assessment information have on her self-esteem and view of herself as a mathematician?*

What do the league tables and SATs results really show?

Data has been published giving secondary school results since 1993 and Key Stage 2 results since 1996. This use of summative assessment information as an indicator of performance is a dangerous one. Of course all schools recognise their accountability to parents, of which the results are one measure. However, they show only the measured attainment levels (as tested through the SATs) and not the progress of children (or value added by the school). This therefore does not take account of where the children started from, nor the changing population of some schools, particularly those located near an armed forces base, those which have a number of traveller children attending, those in deprived areas or those with a high population of refugee families. The only way to provide evidence of the 'value added' dimension is to test the children on entry to the school or Key Stage and then again on exit. Perhaps this is the reason why 'baseline assessment' completed on entry to school as well as Key Stage 1 SATs results become essential as a basis for later comparisons of progress.

All schools now need to set targets for children's progress and report these to their LEA and governing body on a regular basis. These sophisticated tracking mechanisms should result in progress in learning for individuals, small groups and year groups of children if they are being used to inform planning and teaching. However, this may not be the case if the procedures being used are neither explicit nor manageable.

> *'The quality and use of assessment remain the weakest aspect of teaching. Many schools are generating a great deal of assessment data, at considerable cost in terms of time, but are not using it to set work based on the pupils' prior attainment or to set appropriate targets for different groups of pupils.'*
> *(OFSTED 2000, paragraph 25, page 28)*

How can we ensure that our assessment is directed towards promoting learning?

The Assessment Reform Group (1999, page 4) found that improving learning through assessment depends on five key factors:

- the provision of effective feedback to children;
- the active involvement of children in their own learning;
- adjusting teaching to take account of the results of assessment;
- a recognition of the profound influence assessment has on the motivation and self-esteem of children, both of which are crucial influences on learning;
- the need for children to be able to assess themselves and understand how to improve.

Each of these aspects will now be discussed in more detail.

Providing effective feedback to children

For feedback to be effective it must make explicit what has been achieved in the current piece of work but must also provide suggestions for how to improve and what to think about when completing the next piece of related work. Feedback from teachers should avoid comparisons with other children. The 1999–2000 OFSTED report for primary schools noted that marking is usually 'positive and encouraging' but that it failed to give sufficient guidance and direction as to how children can improve. There should be an agreed policy for marking in a school so that children become used to the responses offered by the teachers. Some schools use a mixture of comments and symbols. It is also important to model and share with children ways in which they can respond to one another's work and ideas in similarly specific ways.

Example: *Feedback from teacher: John, I particularly liked the range of vocabulary which you used in your poem today. In your next piece of writing continue to do this but do check the spellings once you have completed the first draft.*

Feedback from child to child: You've used really interesting words in that poem.

The Assessment Reform Group (1999, page 5) also noted that 'greater attention was given to marking and grading, much of it tending to lower the self-esteem of pupils, rather than to providing advice for improvement'.

Involving children actively in their learning

In order to encourage children to become actively involved in their own learning they need to know what it is they are going to learn, why it is important for them to understand this and how it relates to other aspects of their learning or the subject being studied. This requires the teacher to share the learning goals or aims for the sessions and then use the plenary section of the lesson to review the learning for that session. This process is becoming a much more common feature of teaching and contributing to its effectiveness.

Children need to be allowed to make some decisions about the learning activities in which they are engaged, what resources to use and how they might go about this. Reflecting on this process afterwards and learning as a result of that reflection is another important feature of involving children actively in their learning. It is also important to help children make connections in their learning and you should do this as an explicit part of your teaching. This can be achieved by using concept maps, revising the key points and other such strategies. Research by Askew *et al.* (1997) sought to identify key factors which enabled teachers to be effective teachers of numeracy, as defined by their children's learning gains. To achieve this they explored the knowledge and beliefs which underpinned the teaching of a sample of 90 teachers. The most effective teachers they found were those who had the ability to make connections in their own understanding and used this as a central feature of their teaching strategies with children.

Adjusting teaching to take account of the results of assessment

The planning cycle is the process by which teachers identify and address children's learning needs based on formative assessment. Assessment can take place at the beginning and end of this cycle. At the beginning it will be focused on finding out what children already know, can do or understand. This information should then be used to make sure that the next learning experiences planned are meaningful and relevant to the child/children being taught. However, an expanded version of this cycle could be used to highlight the detail of more formalised assessment practices. If it is appropriate, the teacher might record the assessments. These records can then be analysed and used either to report to parents or to set suitable targets for the individual child, small groups of children or even the class.

Target setting has become a significant issue and part of every teacher's practice over the past few years. It has become common practice for teachers to set SMART targets. Targets should be:

Specific (tightly focused)
Measurable (able to be demonstrated and so using active verbs)
Achievable (the next small step)
Realisable or realistic
Time related (achievable within an agreed time frame e.g. half a term)

Example: *To be able to spell 20 keywords correctly when these are called out.*

These targets can then be built into future plans so that the children have a chance to work towards and then meet the targets. This process exemplifies how assessments of different kinds (either formative or summative) should be used to inform teaching and learning.

The assessment cycle in Fig. 2.1 (adapted from Headington 2000, page 5) demonstrates the relationship between assessment and planning and indicates the role of target setting within this process.

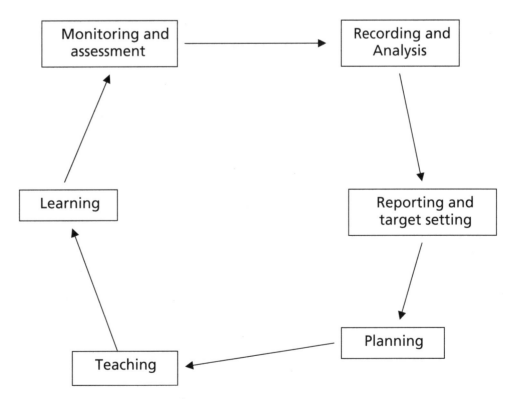

Fig. 2.1   The assessment cycle.

Recognising the profound influence assessment has on the motivation and self-esteem of children

This links with the earlier discussion about relationships and the need to ensure that the pressures of testing procedures and the drive to improve standards do not impinge detrimentally upon the relationship between teachers and children, nor between children themselves.

Developing children's positive motivation towards learning must be an aspiration for all teachers. As adult learners we recognise the power of feeling motivated to learn, find out or challenge ourselves, and the same is true of children. However, the damaging effects that an unmotivated child can have upon a teacher, a class and the ethos that is being fostered within that class are all too apparent in many classrooms. If a child with low attainment is receiving feedback from the teacher which indicates that they lack 'ability', they will of course become demotivated since they believe that they cannot learn. As motivation is a subjective feeling, based on one's experiences, perceptions and expectations, it is the responsibility of the teacher to seek to motivate every individual in the class. This can be challenging and undoubtedly requires skill, imagination, creativity, enthusiasm and above all specific feedback regarding individual children's achievements for behaviour, attitude and work. It also requires a basic acceptance on the part of the teacher that children are different and require high expectations as well as different levels of support. (This is an issue covered in greater detail within the section on 'One school for all', see **pages 61, 91–95, 120**).

Motivating children is also dependent upon setting the correct level of challenge within tasks and the ability to differentiate appropriately is directly linked to the assessment information that a teacher has gathered and is using to guide their planning. If the level of challenge is too high, the child might consider this a risk 'not worth taking', feel helpless and disengage. Conversely, if the challenge is not high enough, boredom and poor motivation might result. This is why it is important for teachers to differentiate tasks appropriately for children.

Enabling children to assess themselves and understand how to improve

Self-assessment is an important life skill to develop. This requires you to monitor and evaluate your learning strategies and achievements by standing back and reflecting on what you have just done or completed. However, children can only assess themselves if they have a sufficiently clear picture of the purpose or targets for their learning. The importance of having a clear view of 'where you are aiming' in any learning activity is reflected in Bruner's theory of instruction cited in his writings (see, for example, Bruner 1966).

This process is clearly linked to fostering independent thinkers and children who are self-motivated and not just reliant upon external reward systems. If this process is modelled and encouraged within a classroom, children should move towards having a sense of ownership of, and a clear idea about how to proceed with, their learning, in other words, what they might do or learn next. The following list of questions is taken from a book by Julie Fisher (2002, page192) and can be used to encourage children to reflect on themselves as learners or on a particular piece of work:

- ➲ What interests me?
- ➲ What do I enjoy doing?
- ➲ What do I want to be able to do?
- ➲ What helps me learn?
- ➲ What would I like to know?
- ➲ Do I know what I want to achieve?
- ➲ Do I think I need help?
- ➲ Do I know who/how to go about getting help?
- ➲ Have I thought how this might be evaluated?
- ➲ How will I evaluate it?

You are now ready to complete the needs analysis linked to this theme in order to know how you might best proceed with your learning.

Assessment

How far have you developed your understanding of assessing and recording children's learning? Reflect on the needs analysis table below and if possible discuss your ideas and your evidence with a colleague, teacher or tutor.

Getting Started	Date/evidence	Developing your Skills	Date/evidence	Extending your Skills	Date/evidence
I am aware of the necessity for providing clear feedback to children about their achievements.		I have read, discussed with the teacher and now understand the school policy on assessment and marking.		I am aware of and have some experience of the statutory requirements for reporting to parents.	
I have observed the ways in which teachers make their expectations for children explicit and reinforce these at the end of a learning activity.		I can involve children in assessing their own learning and incorporate this into my practice.			
When teaching a group of children I can use observation, listening and questioning effectively as assessment strategies.		I can select, plan for and use a range of assessment strategies in my teaching.		I can annotate and level children's work using National Curriculum level descriptions.	
I can evaluate my teaching and reflect on how the children responded to my questioning and expectations for their learning.		I can evaluate the effectiveness of the assessment strategies I use. I am aware of their strengths and limitations.		I understand the need to seek additional information to support the 'best fit' process of levelling children's attainment and know where and how to gather this information.	
I understand the need to make clear my expectations for tasks and the successful completion of these when working with a small group.		I can plan for and involve other adults in the assessment process.		I am able to compare children's attainments from different year groups and use these to inform my teaching.	
I understand and know how to use the assessment information I have gathered to inform my teaching of a small group.		I understand how to use assessment information to inform my future planning for a class.		I understand the target-setting process and the need to use data on children's attainment from a variety of sources to inform my teaching.	
I recognise the key issues when assessing children's learning.		I recognise the need to keep ongoing records on children's learning and can do this in my class.		I am able to discuss children's progress with parents on an informal daily basis as well as during a parents' evening.	
*If one or more of these is not yet ticked, you may find it helpful to complete the activities on **pages 58–60**.*		*If one or more of these is not yet ticked, you may find it helpful to complete the activities on **pages 85–89**.*		*If one or more of these is not yet ticked, you may find it helpful to complete the activities on **pages 115–118**.*	

This section covers issues concerned with inclusion. A number of important debates are outlined and discussed in order to provide you with the relevant background information required to understand the complexity of the events leading up to the current educational focus on inclusion. In this section you will be exploring:

- ➲ the historical context for educating children with differences;
- ➲ disability movement issues and the use of the term inclusion;
- ➲ the differences between religious, medical and social models of disability;
- ➲ the impact of these developments on children, parents and teachers.

A brief outline of the historical context for educating children with 'differences'

Segregated education for those children with mental or physical disabilities was formalised in England through the 1899 Elementary Education Act. Medical officers were appointed to decide whether a particular child should be educated in an ordinary school, in a special school or not at all. The trend from that point until recently has been for most of the educational provision for disabled children and those with more severe learning difficulties to remain segregated and dominated by medically influenced attitudes. (The detail of this medical model of disability is discussed below and contrasted with a social model of disability.) However, this initial Education Act set a precedent for the relationship between impairment and the education of the child and although this has changed in guise and detail through the years, it remains central to the concept of separate special schooling. It might be interesting to ask yourself how many children with disabilities and/or severe learning difficulties you met, worked with and played alongside during your own schooling.

The 1944 Education Act introduced secondary education for all. The '11-plus' was used to select children at age 11 for grammar schools, secondary modern schools or technical schools, although the latter did not develop to the same extent. Local Education Authorities were instructed to make separate provision for those children with an impairment of 'mind or body'. To facilitate this process eleven categories of impairment were introduced, including 'educationally sub-normal', 'delicate' and 'maladjusted'. An enquiry was set up to review special educational provision in schools in 1978, chaired by Mary Warnock. This made a number of recommendations, which were then incorporated into the 1981 Education Act. This new Act abolished categories of handicap and focused on the individual instead of the category of need and thus the notion of 'special educational need' was developed. Another significant development was the introduction of statements of educational need, which specified the required provision for individual children, were linked to funding and reviewed regularly. For the first time, professionals were encouraged to take account of parents' views through this assessment procedure. This Act also promoted the use of 'integration' where possible and this principle will be explored later. There were a number of examples of successful and significant integration in certain parts of the country. However, this was not a consistent picture and the numbers of children in segregated education as a proportion of the school population remained largely unchanged (1.41% in 1977 and 1.35% in 1998, figures taken from page 11, Mason and Rieser 1994).

The 1988 Education Reform Act saw the introduction of a nationally prescribed curriculum, alongside a national testing and assessment framework. Although this theoretically introduced entitlement to a broad and balanced curriculum for all children, which was a major step forward, large numbers of children were still being taught in separate special schools. A number of factors linked to this new

Act resulted in mainstream schools questioning the desirability of having children with special educational needs in the classroom, particularly those with less severe needs, as there was no additional funding to support this. The issues which seemed to concern schools were:

➲ the impact of children with special educational needs on Key Stage 2 test results which were being published;
➲ the additional costs which could be incurred in educating children with special educational needs at a time when funding was being transferred directly to schools;
➲ the attitudes of parents generally to the inclusion of children with special educational needs and the impact this could have on the numbers of children in school and so on the school budget.

Example: *The parents of a child with disruptive behaviour have approached a head teacher in a school and asked to enrol their son in the school. The head teacher thinks very carefully about the impact this might have on the other children in the class and school and what other parents might have to say about this potential disruption.*

The 1993 Education Act placed a duty on the Secretary of State to issue a Code of Practice on the Identification and Assessment of Special Educational Needs and this came into effect in 1994. This introduced a five-stage model as a framework for school-based assessment and intervention. The five stages were related to a continuum of special educational needs which was related directly to a continuum of provision and professional involvement from a variety of services. This meant that the provision of funding and services should be related directly to the needs of the child. The involvement of parents at each stage in the assessment procedure for the Code was seen as a crucial part of the process. It became statutory for all schools to have a named co-ordinator and a written policy for SEN. The rights and duties contained in the 1993 Act have since been consolidated into Part IV of the 1996 Education Act.

Example: *Jonathan is still having difficulties learning to read by the age of seven. A general assistant works with him for 15 minutes every day using a structured reading programme.*

Example: *Helen has severe and general learning difficulties. She has the support of a general assistant working alongside her in the classroom for up to one hour a day.*

The Special Educational Needs and Disability Act 2001 delivers an enhanced right to a mainstream education for children with special educational needs, amends the Disability Discrimination Act 1995 and delivers a range of enforceable rights for disabled children.

The revised SEN Code of Practice came into effect from 1 January 2002 and replaces the previous 1994 Code of Practice. It provides practical advice to LEAs, maintained schools and early education settings regarding their duties to identify, assess and make provision for children's special educational needs. It includes separate chapters on working in partnership with parents, pupil participation and working in partnership with other agencies. The Code of Practice (2002) also recommends that schools and LEAs should adopt a graduated approach to provision through *School Action* and *School Action Plus* and *Early Years Action* and *Early Years Action Plus*.

Part 2 of the Special Educational Needs and Disability Act 2001 has also addressed the recommendations of the Disability Rights Task Force contained within its report From Exclusion to Inclusion (December 1999). This prohibits 'all schools from discriminating against disabled children in their admissions arrangements, in the education and associated services provided by the school for its pupils or in relation to exclusions from school'. The new anti-discrimination duties on LEAs and schools will be more extensively explained in a Disability Rights Code of Practice for schools, prepared by the Disability Rights Commission.

Disability movement issues and the use of the term inclusion

Having considered the historical context for special educational needs it is important to understand the origin and nature of the debate on inclusion. More recently, there has been a growing movement of disabled people campaigning for their human rights and this has focused particularly on educational provision, given the impact this has on an individual's opportunities for the future.

The disability movement has argued that segregated schooling does not equip disabled children with the appropriate skills and opportunities to live a full and active life. Moreover, it largely conditions them to accept considerably devalued social roles and in so doing condemns them to a life of dependence and further isolation.

They have argued instead for an 'inclusive' approach to education. This requires the recognition that impairment, disability and difference are a common experience for many individuals and should therefore be a central issue in the planning and delivery of education. They also argue that this is a very different position from that of earlier forms of integration which were interpreted in a variety of ways, but which all assumed some form of assimilation of the disabled child into the mainstream school, which remained largely unchanged. This fundamentally differs from inclusion, which is about the child's right to belong to their local mainstream school, to be valued for who they are and to be provided with the support they need in order to thrive in the mainstream school. It requires all the children and adults within the school to learn about and respect each and every child's experience.

The following quote is taken from United Nations Educational, Scientific and Cultural Organisation (UNESCO) Salamanca World Statement on Special Needs Education 1994. It has been agreed by representatives of 92 governments and is supported by the present British government.

> 'We ... reaffirm ... the necessity and urgency of providing education for children, youth and adults with special educational needs within the regular education system ...' (paragraph 1)

> '... regular schools with this inclusive orientation ... provide an effective education to the majority of children and improve the efficiency and ultimately cost-effectiveness of the entire education system.' (paragraph 2)

Two other important points need to be made about inclusion. The first is that inclusive education is a process, not a structure, and therefore recognises that communities, schools and individuals will be starting this process from different positions but need to share the journey if the school is to really become inclusive. The second is that inclusive education is not another name for special needs education. Instead it is seen as something more profound than this, with fundamentally different principles underlying it. Its focus is on identifying and minimising the barriers to learning and participation and maximising the resources to support learning and participation. This should be the case for all children and is therefore based on an entitlement to equal opportunities. It might be helpful to consider how this approach can be used therefore to overcome the difficulties faced by any particular groups of children, whether to do with impairment, ethnic origin, language, gender, social class, sexual orientation or other specific groups such as the children of travellers. It is worth remembering that in the past children from such groups have been segregated on the basis of their ethnic origin, disability or gender and for many people this is no longer considered socially acceptable.

What are the differences between religious, medical and social models of disability?

The historically held religious view of disability was based on people's fears and belief that this was 'divine punishment' exercised on human beings. The prevalent medical model of disability focuses predominantly on the diagnosis, labelling and remediation of the impairment (see Fig. 2.2). Intervention is based on 'curing or limiting the effects of' the impairment. This means that medical or other professionals make decisions about the nature of these interventions as well as using this information to determine the nature and degree of support offered and what type of schooling is appropriate. Rarely is the focus on the needs of the person in terms of their holistic development. Decisions taken by professionals about these individual children clearly affect the quality of their day-to-day lives as well as the longer-term opportunities available to them. Many children educated in segregated settings may well go on to find that, as adults, decisions about where they live and work are also taken by professionals rather than themselves.

Example: *Abdul has a hearing impairment. When visiting the bank, he has to take his sister with him in order to communicate with the bank staff seated behind a screen. The medical model sees his impairment as the problem. Abdul says the problem is that his bank is not fitted with a hearing loop.*

A contrasting model (called the social model), and one advocated by many people with disabilities, starts by valuing the child and identifying instead prejudice and discrimination in the institutions, policies, structures and environments of society as the principal reason for exclusion, rather than the impairment of the individual (Mason and Rieser 1994). From this different starting point the child is given a voice to define his or her own strengths and needs, along with those close to them. Central to this approach is the recognition that we are all social beings who need meaningful relationships, irrespective of physical, emotional or intellectual impairments. In order to develop these relationships all children should be allowed to work and play together so that they learn from each other. This is an outcome-based model in which resources (both human and material) are provided for the child rather than the child being required to change and 'fit in'. Appropriate changes can also be made to the physical environment in which the child is working as a way of reducing the barriers to their success, if necessary. It is essentially a problem-solving approach based on collaboration and the building up of inclusive communities (see Fig. 2.2 for both the medical and social models of disability).

Example: *Eleanor uses a wheelchair and needs to travel to the leisure centre. Rather than assume that she has no need to get to the leisure centre on public transport, the social model would argue that all buses should be accessible to wheelchair users. The problem is not Eleanor's disability, it is the fact that buses are not accessible.*

The Medical Model

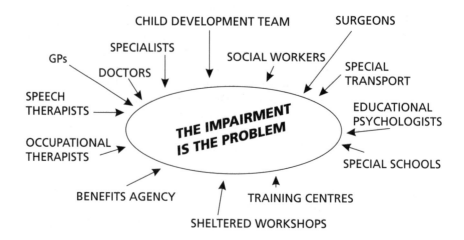

DISABLED PEOPLE AS PASSIVE RECEIVERS OF SERVICES AIMED AT CURE OR MANAGEMENT

The Social Model

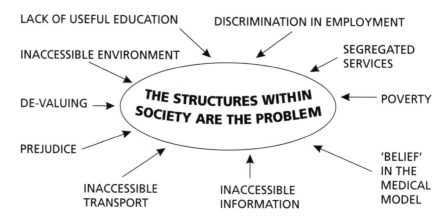

DISABLED PEOPLE AS ACTIVE FIGHTERS FOR EQUALITY WORKING IN PARTNERSHIP WITH ALLIES

© DISABILITY EQUALITY IN EDUCATION

Fig. 2.2 Medical/social models.

What has been the impact of these developments on children?
Until the fairly recent past, children themselves were not seen as participants in the process of assessing and determining their needs. Thankfully, this situation is changing. Teachers and other professionals recognise the benefits of consulting children about their needs and ensuring that they have some ownership of the decisions, plans and strategies used to support their learning and development within school. This will boost their self-esteem and motivate them and is ultimately based on a more respectful relationship between adult and child. Chapter 3 in the new SEN Code of Practice (2001) highlights the importance of children participating in all the decisions about their education and provides guidance for this.

What has been the impact of these developments on parents?
It was through the 1981 Education Act that an important shift began towards consulting and informing parents about the needs of and decisions taken in relation to their child if the child has special educational needs. This was in keeping with a more general shift at the time, which recognised the importance of 'parents as partners' in the education of their children. There is a general trend towards parents

having much more influence upon decisions relating to their child's education. This has also been the case in relation to supporting parents whose children have special educational needs. Various interest groups have developed to 'give parents a voice'. (See the Dyslexia Association, Parents for Inclusion and many others.) Chapter 2 of the SEN Code of Practice (2001) underlines that it is essential for all professionals to be proactive in working with parents and value the contribution they make. It also now requires all LEAs to have a parent partnership service and to offer independent conciliation services. This move appears to recognise the stressful nature and potentially disempowering effect on parents of an education system that continues to deal with the special educational needs of children using a medical model. Many parents feel confused, helpless and sometimes in conflict with a school when trying to support a child with special educational needs.

What has been the impact of these developments on teachers?

It would be fair to say that prior to the introduction of the 1994 Code of Practice many mainstream teachers felt that it was not really their responsibility to monitor and support children with special educational needs. Indeed, teachers were able to turn for support to LEA advisors and other professionals with expertise in the area of special educational needs. However, from this point on, there was an expectation that all classroom teachers, with the support of the special educational needs co-ordinator in the school, would be responsible in the first instance for assessing, supporting and monitoring the progress of most children with special educational needs. For those children with more complex needs or difficulties which persisted despite the school's intervention, other professionals could be called upon to offer advice and guidance. The 1994 Code of Practice made clear which professionals were responsible for monitoring and intervening to support individual children at each stage in the framework.

The majority of children with severe or multiple disabilities continued to be educated outside mainstream schools. It is only since the 1996 Education Act that many more schools have begun to develop expertise in supporting children with more severe special educational needs. The 1996 Act put a general duty on LEAs to secure the education of children with statements in mainstream schools provided that it:

- ⊃ is in line with the parents' wishes;
- ⊃ is suitable for the child's special educational needs;
- ⊃ does not hinder the education of other children;
- ⊃ represents efficient use of resources.

Although these provisos meant that some schools and LEAs were still reluctant to admit children with statements into mainstream schools, the statistical evidence indicates that the number of children with statements who are placed in mainstream schools has increased steadily since 1996.

Data from the DfES Statistics of Education: SEN in England, January 2001 Bulletin (ref 12/2001) indicates some changes in the location of children with statements.

	% of children with statements in maintained mainstream schools	% of children with statements placed in special schools
1996	56% (127 300)	–
2000	60% (152 800)	41%
2001	61% (158 000)	36%

Also over this period the total number of children in special schools (excluding pupil referral units), including those with and without statements, fell from 98 100 to 95 600.

This has resulted in the development of some very successful examples of inclusive practices within individual classrooms, schools and *some* LEAs, although there are wide variations between and within different regions. It is this developing initiative which the latest Special Educational Needs and Disability Act (2001) seeks to consolidate and take further. The emphasis in schools has been shifted even further from procedures to concentration on teaching, learning and achievement of children. Teachers will need to consider many aspects of their teaching practices and take account of the guidance on:

- ⊃ assessment, planning and reviews for individual children;
- ⊃ grouping for teaching purposes;
- ⊃ use of additional human resources;
- ⊃ curriculum and teaching methods.

The impact will be felt directly by many teachers who now need to reflect on their value systems and engage in the process of critically examining what can be done to increase the learning and participation of the diverse population of children within the school and its community.

You are now ready to complete the needs analysis linked to this theme in order to know how you might best proceed with your learning.

Assessment

How far have you developed your understanding of inclusion and equal opportunities issues? Reflect on the needs analysis table below and if possible discuss your ideas with a colleague, teacher or tutor.

Getting Started	Date/ evidence	Developing your Skills	Date/ evidence	Extending your Skills	Date/ evidence
I have read, discussed with the teacher and now understand school policies on SEN, equal opportunities and inclusion.		I recognise the possible effects of race, gender, class and impairment on children's learning and perceptions of themselves.		I am aware of and understand the implications of various statutory acts related to equal opportunities issues and accommodate them within my teaching practices.	
I have identified several examples of these policies in practice around the school.		I can evaluate my teaching strategies to ensure equal access and opportunities.		I know how I can respond to children who demonstrate stereotypical attitudes, racism or sexism.	
I understand the three principles of inclusion in the National Curriculum and can recognise these in practice.		I can identify one aspect of my teaching to improve in relation to equal access and opportunities and specify how I am going to do this.		I continually evaluate my practice against the three principles for inclusion.	
I can evaluate the observations I have made in relation to the principles of inclusion.				I am able to evaluate my own beliefs and practices and engage with other professionals in discussions about these.	
When working with a group of children I can plan for and use at least one of the principles of inclusion.		I have audited the resources available in the classroom in terms of gender, disability, cultural/ethnic, linguistic and religious diversity.		I use a rich range of resources, which represent the diversity of society, as well as teaching approaches which demonstrate an appropriate value system.	
I recognise the key issues within inclusion and am aware of how I might address these within my own teaching.		I have sought to enrich the resources available for learning and teaching in order to take account of gender, disability, cultural/ethnic, linguistic and religious diversity.		I take a pro-active approach to equal opportunities and inclusion issues and plan my teaching to ensure this is a central feature of it.	
*If one or more of these is not yet ticked, you may find it helpful to complete the activities on **pages 61–62**.*		*If one or more of these is not yet ticked, you may find it helpful to complete the activities on pages 90–95.*		*If one or more of these is not yet ticked, you may find it helpful to complete the activities on pages 119–121.*	

This chapter has introduced you to some of the professional aspects of primary teaching which you will need to know and understand in order to become an effective teacher. Having read this chapter and completed the needs analysis process, you should be more aware of your strengths and areas in need of further development. Following the page references of activities in each needs analysis table will help you plan your learning for each theme in Chapters 3, 4 and 5. Do not forget to discuss your training needs, based on what you have learned about yourself through completing this chapter, with your training provider or teacher.

Contents

Introduction

The information and activities in this section are aimed at trainees who are at the beginning of their training. The activities described can be carried out with different age groups, and given that they are related to your general professional practice, can be completed within different subject teaching. For example, you can choose which of the planning activities you are going to complete within different curriculum subject teaching. You will need to link activities together if you are also using the other subject-based books within this series. So do take advantage of the fact that the 'Professional Issues' activities can and should be linked to a range of curriculum subjects. At this level the activities are generally designed to be carried out with a group or individual children. You may also be required to carry out observations of other teachers or children at work and complete some reading, particularly of relevant school policies.

For the purposes of auditing your development during your training you will need to refer to the Standards in DfES/TTA (2002) *Qualifying to Teach – Professional Standards for Qualified Teacher Status*. A summary version of the Standards that can be addressed during different themes is included as an Appendix at the back of this book. Please refer to this regularly. As you complete each piece of evidence that accompanies the activities it is important that you share this with your supervising teacher, school-based mentor and/or training provider tutor, as relevant. This profiling process is an important one but you should be given advice on this from your training provider. Do ensure that you link the completion of the activities in this chapter with the profiling requirements of your training.

The matrix below outlines the content and activities for this chapter. Each theme has been divided into six common elements. Use the summary of the Standards for the Award of Qualified Teacher Status in the Appendix to see how your experiences at this level can contribute directly to the profiling process.

	When finding out about policy and practice in the school	When observing other teachers' practice	When observing children	When planning for a small group	When teaching a small group	When reflecting on your teaching
How do you define yourself in the role of the teacher?	Obtain basic information about the school day, relevant policies, routines and expectations for staff.	Observe and make notes on the nature of the interactions between the staff and the children. Identify the ways in which children's emotional and social needs are being catered for and accommodated within the classroom.		Plan an activity which encourages children to share their ideas and experiences.	Ensure that you present yourself appropriately as a teacher to the children. Establish respectful communication. Ensure that you support and encourage all children so that they contribute.	Establish effective communication systems with the class teacher and other staff. Reflect on what you have learned about children's social and emotional development from your observations. Evaluate the activity you planned for the group and your role in supporting individuals within this.
How do children learn and teachers teach?		Observe teaching in the classroom. Identify the theoretical basis for the teaching approach.				Reflect on the appropriateness of particular approaches across subjects.
How do you create a learning environment?		List rules and routines used in a classroom. Observe how behavioural expectations are made clear and reinforced during a lesson. Observe a lesson focusing on timing and activities.	Observe how the children are accessing, using and taking responsibility for resources.	Plan for the use of established routines and expectations for behaviour.	Employ established routines. Make clear behavioural expectations and how children will know when they have achieved these.	Evaluate which rules and routines work best for you and why.
How do you plan for learning and teaching?	Read curriculum policies for any subject you are going to teach.	Evaluate the teacher's planning to understand its purpose and content.		Plan a lesson with clear learning objectives for a group of children, based on the teacher's medium-term plans.		Evaluate lessons against planned learning objectives for children and your own professional practice.
How do you assess and record children's learning		Observe a teacher's feedback to children and their responses or reactions to this.	Observe how children respond to feedback.	Plan an activity with clear instructions, expectations and questions.	Share the learning objectives and purpose of an activity with children and question them about what they have learned.	Evaluate what you have learned about giving appropriate assessment feedback to children. Reflect on what to make explicit at the outset of an activity and how you provide feedback on children's achievements.
One school for all?	Find and read school policies on SEN, equal opportunities and inclusion. Discuss with teacher.	Identify examples of each policy listed above.	Collect evidence that policies are affecting children's behaviour and learning.		Integrate one of the principles of inclusion when teaching a group.	Consider what you have learned about inclusion and how you might address the principles of inclusion in your own practice.

All the activities in this chapter are outlined in full and have the following information provided with them:

⊃ essential background to the activity, including such items as which equipment to use and which setting might be most appropriate for carrying it out;
⊃ a description of the activity and all the elements that go to make it up;
⊃ ideas on how to evaluate its success;
⊃ suggested further background reading;
⊃ your achievements.

Chapter 3   How do you define yourself in the role of the teacher?

Link to Professional Standards for QTS

Please refer to the Appendix for information about the links between this theme and the Professional Standards for the Award of Qualified Teacher Status.

Becoming a teacher

As a trainee or new teacher you must be aware of the impression you make on colleagues, parents and children. Your first encounters in a school are likely to be with the head teacher, teaching and support staff. Do not underestimate the important role each person plays. You will come to rely on a caretaker who helps you reorganise your classroom, colleagues who share planning responsibilities with you, teaching assistants who work with challenging children and a head teacher who gives advice on job applications and interview techniques. It should go without saying that you are polite, positive and appreciative when working with others in the close-knit community of a school.

You will need to find out about the implicit and explicit codes in the school in order to make a good impression and contribute to the smooth running of everyday life in school. You can learn a great deal about the timing of the school day, policies, routines and expectations for staff by reading documentation. Policies on health and safety, behaviour management and parental partnership will be particularly useful in helping you to understand the day-to-day operation of the school. There may be a staff or student handbook which describes your roles and responsibilities as well as the support available to you. You will need to identify sections which are particularly relevant to you and will inform your work in the classroom.

The way you look and behave should be professional and appropriate at all times. Schools sometimes have a written dress code; with others it is unwritten but fairly clear. Smart, practical clothing gives everyone the impression that you take the job seriously and are ready to get down to business. It is sensible to allow for specialist activities such as PE and bring appropriate clothing and footwear if necessary.

The first few meetings with children are crucial in building the foundations of respectful relationships. These relationships will then develop gradually based on your interactions with individuals and groups. The first meeting with children serves to build the foundations of a positive relationship and establish authority and control. Hayes (1999, pages 19–20) describes this as a three-stage process: 'sparring, courtship and partnership'. At all times during this process of negotiation and compromise you should remain firm, fair and outwardly confident. This will determine boundaries and shared goals.

Preparation
Read Hayes (1999) Chapter 2.

Plan your first meeting with a group of children. Try to put yourself in the position of a child and imagine how he or she will feel and respond. This will help you to meet the children's needs as well as your own. Consider every aspect of the encounter and remember how important first impressions can be. Your plan should include details of your dress, physical position in relation to the children, voice, choice of language, content of spoken communication, body language, facial expressions, expectations of behaviour and learning. Make sure you are clear about how to deal with children who do not respond in the expected manner.

Task

Carry out your first formal meeting with the class. Make sure there are opportunities for the children to contribute and ask questions.

Evaluation and follow up

Evaluate how well you communicated with the children and how much they understood. Identify parts of the encounter that did not go as you expected. Explain why this happened and how you will alter your approach next time you meet the children.

Respectful relationships

Children come to school bringing their widely varying experiences of life and learning. School plays a large and influential role in their lives, but it is by no means the only place where they learn. From the moment they are born children are learning about themselves and the world around them. Schools provide a formal framework for learning. This is open to many influences such as national and local politics, religious organisations, the LEA and the head teacher. Every teacher is the interface between these influences, the curriculum and the children in his or her class.

Widely accepted social constructivist theories, such as those of Vygotsky (1962) and Bruner (1990), assert that learning takes place through social interaction. This emphasises the importance of classroom relationships. It also highlights the need for teachers to plan these social interactions and not leave them to chance. Children need to be taught to collaborate just as they need to be taught to read or add up and of course some will find it easier than others. Where social development is a learning objective for a lesson, it should be made explicit in planning and to the children. Children need opportunities to achieve as individuals and as members of a group. Fisher (1995, page 139) emphasises the importance of 'success in learning for the group and for the individuals within it'.

Preparation

Read Moyles and Robinson (2002) pages 30–35.

Task

Plan and teach an activity to a group of children which provides opportunities for them to share their ideas and experiences. Ensure that you provide support and encouragement for all the children so that they feel confident about contributing. This could be an elicitation activity (see **page 86**) which will inform your future planning and help you to meet their learning, social and emotional needs.

Evaluation and follow up

Evaluate the contribution of each child. Notice which children were more confident and the ways in which each child expressed his or her ideas and experiences. Make brief notes to help you plan the next activity with this group, supporting individuals and encouraging the involvement of each child.

Successful communication

Communication can take many forms, it is not simply what you say and how you say it. Verbal, written, physical (position, movement and posture), facial (use of expressions) communication and listening are all part of the social interactions which occur in classrooms. They are also opportunities to teach and learn and need to be carefully considered to avoid giving mixed messages and causing confusion. Research has shown (Galton *et al.* 1980, Moyles 1992, Pollard *et al.* 1994) that as much as 80% of teachers' time is spent talking with children. This figure does not include all the other communication that is going on at the same time.

Non-verbal forms of communication are powerful in the classroom. The position of the teacher in the room, whether he or she is sitting or standing, an encouraging or admonishing look directed at a specific child or group will all have a significant influence on both individuals and the whole class. For this reason, the trainee should try to be aware of all aspects of communication, observe the ways in which teachers make use of them and plan to vary their own methods of communication when teaching.

Preparation
Read Moyles and Robinson (2002) pages 57–62.

Task
During one lesson, observe and list the nature and frequency of the interactions between the teacher and the children. Notice the variety and effects of these interactions.

Evaluation and follow up
Evaluate the ways in which each interaction relates to the children's learning and wider development. Identify how the teacher is meeting the social and emotional needs of the children through these interactions.

Schools and individual teachers have established routines and rules which facilitate the smooth running of the classroom and maximise children's learning experiences. As a trainee, it is usually best to continue using these systems rather than trying to establish your own. This will minimise any disruption to the class and help to develop a respectful relationship with the teacher. During experiences in a variety of schools and classrooms, you will observe and use a range of techniques. This will help you to establish what works for you and to develop your own style. Similarly, working within the teacher's usual expectations for behaviour and learning will help trainees develop an understanding of their own standards and give the children the security of a consistent approach (see **pages 50–51**).

There will always be questions that you need to ask and points that need clarification. Your teacher is always your first port of call and should be able to answer most of your queries, directing you to others when appropriate. Do not worry unduly about asking a lot of questions to start with. It is always better to ask than to continue, unsure and lacking in confidence. Children will pick up on this quickly and lose faith in your authority. You can create problems for others by not following routines and structures, such as failing to pass on resources to the correct person or being late for an assembly. Keeping people informed is part of working as a team. Colleagues will be much more willing to share their experience with you if you are seen to be getting involved and contributing.

As a trainee, you should demonstrate commitment to teaching and be willing to reflect on and discuss your progress with the teacher. The Standards for the Award of Qualified Teacher Status from the TTA (2002) set out the competencies against which your progress is measured and can be used to set weekly targets in discussion with the teacher. It is important to identify your individual needs and plan for your progress in every lesson that you teach. Opportunities to observe lessons should also be used to focus on specific aspects of teaching relevant to your current stage of development.

Preparation
Read Moyles and Robinson (2002) Chapter 14.

Task
This task is about ensuring good communication with the class teacher. Provide the teacher with information about any previous experience in the classroom and targets that you have set for your development. Work with the teacher to identify your priorities and the ways in which you will both work in the classroom to support your development. Make sure that you always provide the teacher with a copy of lesson or activity plans for groups while you are working within a lesson led by him or her. You will also need to set up a system for communicating individual children's achievements during these lessons. The file containing your lesson plans and resources should be an open, working document always available to the teacher and other observers. It should be well organised, clearly labelled and up to date at all times.

Evaluation and follow up
Review your progress with the teacher every week. Assess your achievements against the targets set and identify areas for further development. This assessment should be used to set targets for the following week.

Now you have read this section and completed the activities you should be able to:

⊃ establish positive relationships with children and staff;
⊃ understand the role and purpose of school policies on health and safety, behaviour management and parental partnership;
⊃ plan to build children's confidence and self-esteem;
⊃ evaluate your success in building children's self-esteem;
⊃ identify the range of forms of communication which are used between teachers and children;
⊃ begin to use a variety of forms of communication, including verbal and non-verbal, in your teaching;
⊃ identify and use classroom routines and rules;
⊃ identify some weekly targets for your development with the teacher;
⊃ evaluate your progress towards these targets and negotiate new ones for the following week.

If you feel that you have completed the tasks successfully, return to the relevant needs analysis and mark it off with the date and evidence. Ask your tutor about being able to use this activity as evidence that you have met the Professional Standards for QTS. Refer to the summary of Standards listed in the Appendix.

Chapter 3 — How do children learn and teachers teach?

Link to Professional Standards for QTS

Please refer to the Appendix for information about the links between this theme and the Professional Standards for the Award of Qualified Teacher Status.

Putting theory into practice

As a trainee teacher you will have a great deal to think about as you begin work in the classroom. You have read about the theoretical basis for learning and teaching, but it is easy to lose sight of this in the hectic school day. In addition, teaching and learning may not fall neatly into experiences that can be classified according to a particular learning theory. Across the course of a week, day or even within one lesson you may see a combination of approaches being used, each of which could be broadly categorised as behaviourist or constructivist.

Example: *Both constructivist and behaviourist theories could influence the teaching of number bonds.*

Jess has ten maths cubes linked together. He has to find as many ways as possible to break the ten into two groups and then record this as a number sentence, for example 5+5=10 or 7+3=10. (constructivist)

A teacher holds up a card with a number on it. The children have to respond as quickly as possible by holding up a card showing the number they would add to it to make ten. (behaviourist)

Preparation
Agree some observation time with your teacher so that you can begin to make links between learning theories and classroom activities.

Task
Observe the activities undertaken in the classroom during a week. Can you identify behaviourist, constructivist or social constructivist approaches within these activities? Reflect on your observations and list five of these activities, briefly describing what you observed and identifying the theoretical basis. Use the table below to help structure your observational notes.

Activity	What is happening?	What is the theoretical basis?

Evaluation and follow up
In your evaluation of these activities think about the following questions:

- How does the learning and teaching relate to the learning theories discussed above?
- Which approaches are used?
- Are particular approaches associated with particular lessons or subjects?
- Are they appropriate to the learning taking place?
- Do you consider any of the approaches to be used inappropriately?

- ⊃ How could another approach be used?
- ⊃ How might it be more successful?

The background to the introduction of the current National Curriculum (2000) was outlined in Chapter 2. Within this the subjects are organised into separate programmes of study for each Key Stage. These outline the broad areas which are to be covered. Attainment in the National Curriculum is set out in eight levels, which relate to the four Key Stages. For five to eleven-year-olds in Key Stages 1 and 2, the expected attainment is:

- ⊃ Key Stage 1: 5–7 years – expected average attainment level two;
- ⊃ Key Stage 2: 7–11 years – expected average attainment level four.

Very able children may work beyond these attainment levels. Separate descriptions for each subject state the expected attainment at each level (see Chapter 2, on how to assess and record children's learning, **pages 24–30**).

Preparation
The influence of social constructivist theories underpins much of the National Curriculum. Look at the programmes of study for science in the Key Stage you are working in for examples of this.

Task
In each subject document find an example of a constructivist or social constructivist approach and complete the middle column of the following table:

Subject	Example	Implications for my teaching
English	En1 (4a) Use language & actions to explore & convey situations, characters & emotions.	Use role play & discussion across the curriculum.
Mathematics		
Science		
Design & technology		
ICT		
History		
Geography		
Art & design		
Music		
Physical education		

Evaluation and follow up
Identify an aspect of the curriculum, and think about the implications for teaching this, using a social constructivist approach. You might ask yourself the following questions:

- ⊃ What are the implications in terms of the way I present information to the children?
- ⊃ What is the balance between providing information and the children finding things out for themselves?
- ⊃ How will I organise the class? What is the balance between whole class teaching, group work and working as individuals?
- ⊃ What are the implications for assessment?
- ⊃ What resources do I need?
- ⊃ What experiences should I provide for the children?

Having thought about these questions, complete the third column in your table. In the example given above you might consider the following:

Subject	Example	Implications for my teaching
History	Hi 4a KS2 How to find out about the events, people & changes studied from an appropriate range of sources of information including ICT based sources.	I will need to provide documents and artefacts relating to WW2. I will need to update my subject knowledge about WW2 so that I can provide important background information to introduce the topic. I will need to ask some key questions which the children can research and investigate using books and other resources. Is there anyone in the community who was a child during WW2 who could come and talk about their experience? How should I prepare the children for this visit? The children could work in groups on a role play to show what they have learned.

Your achievements

Now you have read this section and completed the activities you should be able to:

➲ recognise that there is a range of theories of learning that influence teaching approaches;
➲ understand the way that theories of learning have influenced curriculum development;
➲ identify the theoretical basis for classroom activities;
➲ recognise the implications of theories of learning for your own practice;
➲ understand the need to provide a range of activities for children;
➲ understand the need to provide a balance between offering information and allowing children to find things out for themselves.

If you feel that you have completed the tasks successfully, return to the relevant needs analysis and mark it off with the date and evidence. Ask your tutor about being able to use this activity as evidence that you have met the Professional Standards for QTS. Refer to the summary of Standards listed in the Appendix.

Chapter 3 — How do you create a learning environment?

Link to Professional Standards for QTS

Please refer to the Appendix for information about the links between this theme and the Professional Standards for the Award of Qualified Teacher Status.

Routines and rules

Teachers establish routines in the classroom to ensure that learning, transitions and change are efficient and manageable. In order for these routines to work, everyone must follow them. To achieve this, teachers usually involve children in choosing the routines and spend some time helping them understand why they are necessary. By setting a good example themselves and providing the children with oral and visual reminders, teachers can establish routines which become part of the normal pattern of behaviour and interaction in the classroom. Investment of time and energy into establishing routines pays off later.

In the classroom there are many mechanisms which can be used to remind children of routines. Children need to be informed. Teachers often find it useful to have a notice board which alerts children to changes and reminds them of regular events, helping them to take responsibility and develop self-discipline. Similarly, ensuring that cupboards, drawers and storage areas are clearly labelled will facilitate children working independently and taking control of their learning. Teachers often encourage children to act more responsibly through assigning roles, such as monitors, to individuals or small groups for short periods of time. These responsibilities should be shared out equally amongst all members of the class.

As a trainee, you will need to learn and use these routines and rules from the start. This will minimise disruption to the class and assist in smoothly integrating you into the social world of the class.

Preparation
Read Moyles and Robinson (2002) pages 41–43 and MacGrath (2000) pages 6–14.

Task
Observe the teacher, perhaps at the beginning or end of the day or during a particular lesson. Make a list of the routines that are used.

- ⮑ What are they?
- ⮑ How do the children know what to do?
- ⮑ Which involve the organisation of the children?
- ⮑ Which involve the organisation of resources?
- ⮑ How do they contribute to the smooth running of the lesson?
- ⮑ How do adults play a part?

Plan and teach a lesson, or part of a lesson, to a group of children. Plan the use of class routines and structures.

Evaluation and follow up
Identify which routines worked best for you and explain why.

Expectations

Children need to feel secure and confident in order for learning to take place. They need to understand what is expected of them in terms of their work and their behaviour. A strict teacher is often well liked and has positive relationships with the children in his or her class, providing that he or she is fair and consistent. Rules, rewards and sanctions must be clear to the children and applied consistently.

Every lesson taught should have learning objectives for the children. These should be kept specific and achievable. Learning objectives should be shared with the class at the beginning of each lesson so that the children know what is expected of them. This need not be a formal announcement but rather should form part of an introduction that stimulates the children's interest and motivates them to investigate, explore and discuss the content of the lesson. You may find it helpful to write learning objectives in 'child-friendly' vocabulary to help them understand, to avoid the need for lengthy explanations and to make objectives more accessible to children. Knowing what is expected and providing a time scale for each activity allows children to take some responsibility for their learning and encourages self-discipline. For most children, reminding them about the expectations for behaviour will help keep them focused.

Preparation

Read Pollard (1997) pages 244–46 and Cowley (2001) Chapter 1.

Discuss the plan for a specific lesson with the class teacher. Establish what the behavioural expectations are and how they are to be achieved.

Task

Observe the lesson, noticing the ways in which the expectations are made clear at the start and how they are reinforced throughout the lesson.

Plan and teach a lesson, or part of a lesson, for a group. Include clear expectations for behaviour. Plan the communication of your expectations, establish rewards and remind the children where appropriate during the lesson.

Evaluation and follow up

Evaluate the extent to which behavioural expectations were met. Identify the ways in which your expectations helped the children's learning and which aspects of the lesson you would change in the future.

Timing

Within each lesson, time spent on different activities needs consideration. The organisation of the literacy hour and daily mathematics lesson provides a model which includes whole class, group and individual work, using visual, aural and kinaesthetic teaching and learning styles. You may find that elements of this model are used across the curriculum to provide structure and variation within lessons.

The rhythm of each lesson and each day should provide opportunities for children to learn in different ways. Using a variety of teaching and learning styles will help to stimulate and motivate the children, but the classroom will need to be organised in such a way that this is possible without disruptive periods of change.

Preparation

Read Kyriacou (1991) Chapter 4.

Task

Observe a lesson focusing on the timing and types of activities.

- ➲ What are the recognisable sections?
- ➲ How and why do they vary in length?
- ➲ How does the teaching style change?
- ➲ How does the learning change?
- ➲ How does the teacher move from one section to the next?

Evaluation and follow up

How does the structure affect children's learning? How appropriate are the activities and timings for the age group?

Resources

Children need to feel safe and comfortable in order to be able to work and learn. They need access to appropriate space and resources and with this, they need to develop some responsibility for their environment.

The teacher is in loco parentis and therefore responsible for the safety of every child in the class. The classroom environment should facilitate learning and ensure that children are safe. Danger can be caused by badly placed furniture, electrical appliances, gas heaters, medicines, dangerous substances, sharp or broken objects. The teacher must ensure that all steps have been taken to avoid these dangers through careful organisation of the classroom and familiarity with regulations and the school health and safety policy. This policy will cover matters of safety and first aid in detail.

Children also need to feel some security and ownership of their own space. If they feel they have had some input into the choice of this space, they will generally take more responsibility for it. Their belongings should be clearly labelled and safely stored, for both practical and personal reasons.

Resources which are used by all the children should be readily available and clearly labelled. The use of these resources should follow established and agreed rules and routines to ensure that they are available for all children when required. Encouraging independent learning involves allowing children to make choices about the resources they need, but this can cause disruption. The teacher may decide to put regularly used equipment, such as pencils, rulers and dictionaries, on tables to avoid too much movement around the class. Teachers often find it useful to train children to look after their resources, encouraging collaboration and responsibility.

Preparation
Read Cowley (2001) Chapter 10.

Task
Make a list of the resources which children use during one lesson. This could include furniture and fixtures as well as smaller equipment such as books and pencils. Divide the list into resources which are available at all times, perhaps on the children's tables, those which are available from elsewhere and those which must be requested from the teacher.

Evaluation and follow up
➲ How are these resources organised?
➲ Who has responsibility for their upkeep?
➲ How do the resources support learning?
➲ What safety issues occur and how are dangers overcome?

Your achievements

Now you have read this section and completed the activities you should be able to:

➲ familiarise yourself with classroom routines and rules;
➲ use established classroom routines and evaluate their effectiveness;
➲ plan and share objectives for behaviour with a group of children;
➲ evaluate the extent to which children meet your expectations;
➲ recognise the structured sections of a lesson and evaluate how these affect children's learning;
➲ identify the resources used in lessons and the ways in which they are organised.

If you feel that you have completed the tasks successfully, return to the relevant needs analysis and mark it off with the date and evidence. Ask your tutor about being able to use this activity as evidence that you have met the Professional Standards for QTS. Refer to the summary of Standards listed in the Appendix.

Chapter 3 How do you plan for learning and teaching?

Link to Professional Standards for QTS

Please refer to the Appendix for information about the links between this theme and the Professional Standards for the Award of Qualified Teacher Status.

Where to start

When you begin working in a primary classroom you will probably focus first on observing the teacher and then on working with a group of children, assisting them with activities planned for them by the teacher. Your first experience of planning your own teaching is likely to be preparing work for one or more groups of children, either for all or part of a lesson. It is important to recognise how your work with a group fits into the planned work for the class as a whole, over the longer term. You should take time to become familiar with the planning which has been done in preparation for the teaching and learning which is going on in the class.

Preparation

Ask your teacher if you can look at the planning which he or she is using as the basis for teaching. This may include daily, weekly or medium-term planning. It may be set out in an agreed format which is used throughout the school. Alternatively, some of the planning may be recorded more informally, in note form.

Task

Ask yourself the following questions:

- What does the teacher hope that the children will learn?
- What inference can you draw from this about the children's current knowledge or understanding?
- Are different levels of attainment identified within the learning objective/s?
- What links are there between the learning objectives, the planned activities and the children's attainment?
- How does the content of the teaching relate to the National Curriculum, to National Strategies or to Schemes of Work (the school's own, the QCA or commercial schemes)?
- How will the lesson/s be organised?
- Is there any new or specialist vocabulary that will be introduced?
- What are the important questions the teacher will ask?
- What resources will the teacher or the children use?
- How will any adult support be used?
- How is ICT being used to support teaching or learning?

You may not be able to answer all of these questions from what is recorded in the planning, but you will need all of this information when you come to plan your own teaching. Experienced teachers may work from planning which is much less detailed than you will need, so you may need to ask the teacher about specific aspects of their planned lessons.

Evaluation and follow up

Reflect on what you have learned about the planning process by reading the teacher's planning. Ask yourself the following questions:

- Where is the content of the planning drawn from?
- What is the purpose of the planned activities?
- What are the stages in the planning process?

Devising a lesson plan

Within a lesson plan you will need to cover the following areas:

- ⊃ date and time of the lesson;
- ⊃ title of the lesson;
- ⊃ previous assessment information;
- ⊃ learning objectives;
- ⊃ vocabulary;
- ⊃ resources;
- ⊃ organisation, including the use of ICT where appropriate;
- ⊃ differentiation;
- ⊃ assessment.

Previous assessment information

At this point you will need to write a brief summary of any assessment information you have prior to this lesson related to individuals, groups or the class as a whole. This important information should provide a reminder to you of issues you need to follow up in the lesson and learning that should be addressed explicitly.

Objectives for the children's learning

Learning objectives for the children (sometimes referred to as learning outcomes) must be clear and specific. These are based on the knowledge, skills or understanding which form the focus of the lesson. They may include aspects of children's social and personal development as well as cognitive or skills objectives. They should not simply be a statement of the task the children will complete. For example, a learning objective is much better expressed as 'the children will recognise the difference between loud and soft sounds' rather than 'the children will play percussion instruments loudly and softly'.

Look at the following statement, which is an objective from the National Numeracy Strategy:

> 'Pupils should be taught to describe and classify common 3-D and 2-D shapes according to their properties.'

This is too complex a learning objective to cover in one lesson, and you would have to break it down into a number of more specific objectives. The following are **not** useful objectives as they do not tell you what the children are going to learn:

- ✗ The children will know about 3-D shapes.
- ✗ The children will cut out circles and triangles.

It would be much more helpful to express the learning objectives in terms such as these:

- ✓ The children will collect examples of prisms and cylinders and match them to name labels.
- ✓ The children will recognise a shape by touch and be able to describe it.

Learning objectives should express exactly that, what the children will *learn*. The more clearly focused your learning objectives, the more useful they will be to you when teaching.

Objectives for your professional development

As a trainee teacher it is also helpful to include one or more objectives based on your professional development, drawn from the Standards for the Award of QTS (see Appendix). Do not try to focus on too many of these at once – pick one or two that you will be able to address during this lesson. By including them in your lesson plan they will become an integral part of the planning for the lesson and so you are much more likely to be able to focus on them effectively in your teaching.

Key questions and vocabulary

Think about the key questions you will need to ask to elicit children's knowledge or support and develop their understanding. What vocabulary will you need to revise or introduce? If you have thought this through in advance you are much less likely to use vocabulary or forms of expression that the children do not understand. Important vocabulary and key questions should be recorded on your lesson plan.

Resources

What resources will you need for the topic and what resources will the children use? Do you need to reserve shared equipment (such as audio visual, science, technology or music resources) or borrow them from another class? Have you got the books and pictures you need? Do you need to make any resources? This is discussed in more detail on **page 52**.

Organisation and structure of the lesson

In planning the way the lesson will be organised you need to think about the timing of different parts of the lesson, the overall content and sequence, how the children will be grouped and how you and any other adults in the class will be employed. The structure will include the introduction and main teaching input, follow-up activities, and summary or plenary sections to consolidate learning at the end of the lesson. Think about how you will introduce the lesson.

- ↻ How will you capture the children's attention and interest at the beginning?
- ↻ How will you make the learning objective clear to them?
- ↻ What are the main teaching points you want to communicate?

You will need to make some notes in your lesson plan of the main points to cover and it may be a good idea to 'rehearse' these as you plan. Try to avoid writing a lengthy 'script' of what you intend to say as this can lead to a rather wooden delivery in the classroom.

- ↻ What will be the follow-up activities for the children? You will need to consider the implications for organisation when planning these.
- ↻ How will you bring the lesson to an end and revise the main teaching points?
- ↻ Will the children be able to show or present the results of their work to others?

When planning the activities the children will complete, try to devise tasks that will motivate them and engage their interest. At this stage in your training, it is likely that you will be working with a group, and all of the children will be undertaking the same task, with you there to support them. Try to make sure that they will be actively involved in their learning tasks.

One difficulty for inexperienced teachers is estimating how long it will take for children to complete a task. Something you have spent a long time planning and preparing may be finished in a few minutes, so it is always a good idea to plan a follow-up activity for early finishers or to challenge more able children further. If the activity is too difficult or too formal for the children, they may become frustrated, bored and demotivated. Bear in mind that children have differing learning and preferred sensory styles, so consider this when planning activities. You may not be able to vary the activities within a single lesson for a group, but you can vary the teaching approaches over time.

Differentiation

Are there different learning objectives, teaching strategies or tasks to meet the needs of children based on their current attainment? How will other adults be involved in supporting differentiation?

Differentiation generally falls into three types: by outcome, by task or by process.

- ↻ Differentiation by outcome: all of the children complete the same task, but the work produced varies according to the different level of attainment in that aspect of the curriculum. For example, following a class discussion and having looked at pictures, leaves and autumn fruits, the children all write a poem about autumn.
- ↻ Differentiation by task: the children are set different tasks designed to cater to their individual needs. Sometimes they can be assigned different roles in a collaborative task, based on their individual strengths or interests. Sometimes the task is similar, but children are asked to respond to it at different levels of complexity. In retelling the story of Cinderella, some children draw a storyboard, some write a simple narrative and some rewrite it in a modern setting.
- ↻ Differentiation by process: the working process is differentiated so as to meet children's needs. This could involve providing additional explanation, additional time to complete the task, providing adult support or targeting an individual or group with extra time during the working session.

Assessment of children's learning

At the end of the lesson you will need to make some assessment of whether the members of the group have met the learning outcome. This may be done formally, for example by marking a piece of writing, or informally by talking to them about what they have done. Whichever approach you adopt, you will need to make some evaluation of whether they have learned what you set out to teach them. It is important to identify those children who have not met the learning objectives and those who have exceeded them.

Evaluation of your learning

In order to support your developing professional practice it is vital that you evaluate your lessons and the planning that underpins them. Try to be as honest and specific as possible in your evaluation of the lesson. Make brief notes about whether the lesson was successful in meeting its objectives and, if not, why you think it was unsuccessful. Think about ways you might change what you do in future. It is not necessary to write a long description of what happened – it is much more useful to use the time reflecting on whether the learning objectives were met and making brief comments to support your planning in future. Evaluate your developing professional skills against the objectives that you set for your teaching.

You will need to devise a format for recording all of this information. A possible layout is provided below. Alternatively, you may be asked to use the school's format. When you are starting out as a teacher you will need to plan in as much detail as possible; this is what will give you confidence in the classroom

Lesson evaluation

Evaluation of children's learning

Children who surpassed the learning objectives	
Name	Extension work required

Children who did not achieve the learning objectives	
Name	Area of concern

Evaluation of student's learning

This section should relate to the target(s) which you set for your own development for this lesson. These should also be linked to your weekly professional targets.

Other issues arising from the lesson in relation to your own practice

This section should identify what you did that helped the children achieve the learning objectives **or not**. You should identify what you have learned and what action you will take as a result of this in the next/future lessons. This might relate to new targets/standards that you need to address. (Use bullet points rather than descriptive text.)

Preparation

Based on your understanding of clear learning objectives and in agreement with your teacher, plan a lesson for a group of children, based on an aspect of the work they are due to cover. Read through the school's policy for teaching that subject and look at the teacher's medium-term planning or the school's scheme of work to establish the broad outline. Use the information above to structure your lesson plan.

Task

Teach the planned lesson to a group of children. Evaluate whether the children have met the learning objectives and how well you met the objective for your professional development. Ask yourself:

- Did the children learn what I hoped to teach them, including any new or specialist vocabulary?
- Were there any aspects which were not understood, and if so, how will I address that in future?
- Were the children actively engaged in the lesson? Was there sufficient/too little/too much work for them to complete?
- Were the tasks sufficiently challenging?
- Did I have all the resources I needed?
- Did I meet the objective I set out for my professional development?

Based on your evaluation either:

- bear in mind what you have learned about the children and your skill as a teacher when you plan the next lesson for the group; or
- refine and amend your lesson plan and teach the same topic to a different group of children in the class or year group. Evaluate the teaching and learning with the new group.

Your achievements

Now you have read this section and completed the activities you should be able to:

- understand the different types of planning undertaken by teachers, its content, structure and purpose;
- recognise the importance of planning carefully for teaching;
- use your knowledge of children's current understanding to plan individual lessons for a group of children;
- understand that objectives should relate to what is being learned rather than to the activity being undertaken;
- construct lesson plans which have clear objectives for children's learning;
- identify learning objectives for your professional development;
- plan lessons which have a clearly defined structure, content, vocabulary, key questions and assessment strategies;
- teach a group of children and evaluate your lesson;
- refine and amend your planning in the light of your lesson evaluation.

If you feel that you have completed the tasks successfully, return to the relevant needs analysis and mark it off with the date and evidence. Ask your tutor about being able to use this activity as evidence that you have met the Professional Standards for QTS. Refer to the summary of Standards listed in the Appendix.

How do you assess and record children's learning?

Link to Professional Standards for QTS

Please refer to the Appendix for information about the links between this theme and the Professional Standards for the Award of Qualified Teacher Status.

What is formative assessment?

'Formative assessment involves the piecing together of planned and incidental assessments to plan and provide for the successful learning of each child.' (Ebbutt 1996, page 143)

Assessment is about trying to gather information about a child's skills, knowledge and understanding. It is a continuous process through which the teacher should extend, challenge or reinforce learning, as appropriate.

Teachers are bound to use intuitive judgements about children gained through their daily interactions with them at work and play. However, gathering evidence in order to refine these judgements should support these intuitive views. This is essential, given the research findings which link teacher expectations to children's performance. This suggests that children whom the teacher expects to do well generally do perform better and vice versa. This process of gathering of information can produce some unexpected results which might surprise a teacher. It can also serve to increase the rigour with which a teacher investigates the boundaries of a child's learning. This is helpful both when a child is causing concern and for a very high-attaining child.

Beginning to develop some formative assessment strategies

There are a number of strategies which can be used for collecting this information and you will need to become proficient in using these within your teaching. At this stage we are going to concentrate on the following.

Observation
There are different types of observation. At one end of the continuum the teacher should simply observe, without intervening or interrupting in any way. At the other end the teacher may be observing but still participating in some kind of interaction with children. All forms of observation can provide useful information about what children do, how they go about their work and interact with each other. When recording observations it is always important to note something about the context in which the observation took place. However, observation alone might not enable the teacher to gain access to their thinking or reasoning unless this happens to be apparent. This is why it is very important for teachers to develop the skills of listening and *really* hearing what it is that children are saying to them rather than what they *think* the children are saying.

Listening
This is an active process and needs to be practised and refined. It is all too easy to offer some kind of comment, question or even non-verbal expression which will interrupt the communication and alter the nature of the interaction taking place. It is easy to forget how much children want to please their teacher and so spend a lot of time and energy trying to work out what it is the teacher wants them to say or do. There is a wealth of literature which indicates that young children are very aware of the power dynamics in a classroom and will alter what they say or do to please an adult or if they are feeling unsafe or challenged by an adult (Holt 1982; Gardner 1993).

Questioning

In order to enhance the evidence gained from observation it is sometimes necessary to question children to elicit their ideas, views or explore their thinking and understanding in greater depth. However, there are different types of questions which teachers can ask children depending on their intentions:

➲ What is 8 times 8?
➲ What is the time now?
➲ How do you spell the word …?

These are called closed questions since they provide only one correct response.

Another category of question is open questions. These encourage a range of responses such as:

➲ How did you do that?
➲ Tell us about what you found out.
➲ Why do you think you arrived at that answer?
➲ What do you think the author was trying to convey through this piece of speech?
➲ What might you like to investigate/find out about next?

A third category of question has been identified through the National Numeracy Strategy (1999) called probing questions. These are specifically planned and worded to find out about children's errors and diagnosing possible difficulties.

Example: *Reception-level question: I'm thinking of a number that looks the same when you turn it upside down. What could it be?*

Example: *Year 4-level question: Tell me a number that has no remainder when you divide it by 2, 3 or 5. Are there any others?*

With all types of questioning for assessment purposes it is important to plan the questions carefully and then ensure that you provide children with long enough to consider and respond. Do not be tempted to answer for them or rephrase the question, as this can be distracting for the child. A generally accepted guideline is to allow four seconds for a response.

For further information on questioning, refer to **pages 73–74**. The issues to do with questioning in specific subject areas will be considered in greater detail in the subject texts which also form part of this series.

Developing individual profiles of children (including personal, social, health and emotional well being) as well as academic issues
It is very important to recognise that children are social beings and learn and play in a variety of contexts, which sometimes lead them to behave in different ways. Therefore it is essential that teachers collect a full picture of each child in their class. This will include information about them across different subject areas as well as their attitudes to learning, likes, dislikes, friendships and so on. The detail of these profiles is important so that the teacher can respond appropriately, modify the curriculum as necessary, make a positive relationship with the child and motivate them to do their best.

Issues to do with confidentiality
As a trainee teacher you need to be aware of issues to do with confidentiality. All written records on individual children need to be recorded using appropriate language so that they are free of judgements and can be shared with parents and carers, as well as other professionals, if required. Try to use specific examples or actual evidence of attainment and avoid making judgements on children's behaviour, potential ability and so on.

Example: *'Claire seems to have some difficulties sharing toys with other children and needs support to do this gently.'*

NOT: *'Claire always snatches toys from other children and behaves spitefully towards them.'*

Preparation and task

In this activity, you will be observing children's responses and listening to the verbal feedback provided for children during a teaching session.

Carry out a timed observation of the teacher you are working with and the feedback he or she provides for children when teaching. Listen to their comments and observe the children's faces, reactions and so on. Make a record of this observation on a schedule like the one below.

Time	Observations and/or comments made by teacher and children	Who?

Evaluation and follow up

How did the children seem to respond? Evaluate what you have seen and listened to and consider how you can provide appropriate assessment feedback to children whilst still protecting their dignity. What strategies will you be seeking to use within your teaching?

Preparation

Plan an activity to be carried out by a small group of children in any area of the curriculum. Try to make clear on your plans, and then to the children themselves, what the purpose of this activity is, the specific learning objectives and how they will know when they have been successful at it or have completed it well. Plan some questions which can be used at the end of the activity to check the children's learning against the identified objectives.

Task

Introduce the activity and then send the children off to start. Shortly into the task (about five minutes later) ask if they are clear about what they have been asked to do and how they will know whether they have been successful. Make a note of their comments. Check this again ten minutes later. Question the children at the end of the task about what they have learned. Use your prepared questions to elicit information about their learning.

Evaluation and follow up

Ask yourself:

- Were there any surprises in relation to what you wanted them to learn or expected them to achieve?
- Were you surprised by what the children said to you?
- Why might they have responded in this way?
- How do you think their responses are influenced by previous tasks/encounters they have had with you?
- Did the questions you had planned enable you to find out about their learning?
- If not, how would you adapt these next time?

Consider what you have learned through this experience about being very specific about the purpose and aim of an activity, sharing clear expectations of outcomes and how you will provide feedback to children about their achievements at the end of a task.

Your achievements

Now you have read this section and completed the activities you should be able to:

- understand the nature and purpose of formative assessment;
- employ the strategies of observation, listening and questioning in order to gather formative assessment information;
- understand the issues related to confidentiality and the nature of the records you keep on children;
- evaluate the nature and quality of the feedback provided by a teacher to children about their achievements;
- plan and deliver some teaching for a group, making clear your expectations for their learning;
- evaluate the success of this teaching activity in relation to your expectations.

If you feel that you have completed the tasks successfully, return to the relevant needs analysis and mark it off with the date and evidence. Ask your tutor about being able to use this activity as evidence that you have met the Professional Standards for QTS. Refer to the summary of Standards listed in the Appendix.

Chapter 3 One school for all?

Link to Professional Standards for QTS

Please refer to the Appendix for information about the links between this theme and the Professional Standards for the Award of Qualified Teacher Status.

Essential background
It will be important for you to take the opportunity at this stage in your training to observe carefully the policies and practices within the school in which you are working which relate to equal opportunities, inclusion and special educational needs. Through these observations and your subsequent discussions with children, teachers, support or classroom assistants and parents you will need to reflect upon the implications of your beliefs and practices.

Preparation
Find and read the school policies on special educational needs, equal opportunities and inclusion (if the latter is in place). Make notes on the key issues within these. Discuss with your teacher how he or she feels the policies are implemented within the school and elicit his or her views on these issues.

Task
Can you find examples of these policies in practice around the school and/or in the playground? Write down two or three examples.

Now read the three principles of inclusion in the National Curriculum (page 30) and find two examples under each of the three headings in the classroom in which you are working. The first example can be taken from your observation of the teacher's practice and the second example from something you have tried to initiate when working with a group of children. It is important that you discuss with the teacher the reasons behind what he or she is attempting to achieve in the example you observe.

Create a table like the one below to help you record these.

Principle for inclusion	Example 1 Initiated by your teacher	Example 2 Initiated by yourself
Setting suitable learning challenges		
Responding to children's diverse learning needs		
Overcoming potential barriers to learning and assessment for individuals and groups of children		

Evaluation and follow up
Now review what you have observed and tried to initiate yourself. Indicate how successful you feel this was in terms of ensuring that the principles of inclusion were adhered to. If these were not successful examples of practice, indicate why not and what you would do differently next time.

Now you have read this section and completed the activities you should be:

⮞ familiar with the school policies on special educational needs, equal opportunities and inclusion;

⮞ able to identify examples of these policies in practice around the school;

⮞ familiar with the three principles of inclusion in the National Curriculum and able to identify examples of these in practice in the classroom;

⮞ able to review and reflect upon your attempts to adopt these principles of inclusion whilst working with a group of children.

If you feel that you have completed the tasks successfully, return to the relevant needs analysis and mark it off with the date and evidence. Ask your tutor about being able to use this activity as evidence that you have met the Professional Standards for QTS. Refer to the summary of Standards listed in the Appendix.

You have begun to develop specific aspects of your professional knowledge, understanding and skills across all the themes covered. By the end of this chapter, the combination of your reading and the classroom-based activities will have provided you with a good foundation upon which to build. It is essential that you check that you have evidence to support all the statements within the needs analysis table at this level and that you have also cross-referenced this to the Standards required for QTS in the Appendix. It is important to talk to your teacher about your progress at this stage. He or she will also be able to help you check that you have appropriate evidence to audit your progress against the Standards through the needs analysis table. However, you will also need to ensure that you have started to complete the profiling required by your training provider since this may cover additional Standards.

Contents

The information and activities in this section are aimed at trainees who are some way through their training and have begun to take responsibility for the whole class for substantial periods of time. Some of you will already have worked through the Getting Started chapter and activities outlined earlier in this book. However, you may start your learning at this chapter because you have already had considerable experience of working in different teaching settings or have worked as a learning support assistant. Alternatively you may feel confident in your understanding of the issues within a particular theme having completed the needs analysis exercise covered in Chapter 2. The activities described can be carried out in a range of primary settings, with different age groups and, given that they are related to your general professional practice, can be completed within different subject teaching. For example, you can choose which of the assessment activities you are going to complete within different curriculum subject teaching. You will need to link activities if you are also using the other subject-based books within this series. So do take advantage of the fact that the professional issues activities can and should be linked to a range of different curriculum subjects. In this chapter, the activities are generally designed to be carried out with a whole class or when you are responsible for teaching and managing several groups in the class at the same time.

For the purpose of auditing your development during your training you will need to refer to the Standards in DfES/TTA (2002) *Qualifying to Teach – Professional Standards for Qualified Teacher Status*. A summary version of the Standards that can be addressed during different themes is included as an Appendix at the back of this book. Please refer to this regularly. As you complete each piece of evidence that accompanies the activities it is important that you share this with your supervising teacher, school-based mentor and/or training provider tutor, as relevant. This profiling process is an important one but you should be given advice on this from your training provider. Do ensure that you link the completion of the activities in this chapter with the profiling requirements of your training.

The matrix below outlines the content and activities for this chapter. Each theme has been divided into six common elements. Use the summary of the Standards for the Award of Qualified Teacher Status in the Appendix to see how your experiences at this level can contribute directly to the profiling process.

	When finding out about policy and practice in the school	When observing other teachers' practice	When observing children	When planning for the class	When teaching a class	When reflecting on your teaching
How do you define yourself in the role of the teacher?	Find out about the school's policy and practice in relation to parents.	Observe and make notes on how the teacher presents themselves to the children. Consider how they use verbal and non-verbal approaches to communicate. Observe how children's individual achievements are recognised and celebrated.		Plan to use teaching strategies that motivate children and build self-esteem.	Communicate your expectations for the children's learning and behaviour clearly at the start of every lesson. Highlight and celebrate achievements against these at the end of every lesson.	Evaluate how successful you have been in motivating children and building their self-esteem. Set targets for your development in discussion with the teacher.
How do children learn and teachers teach?	Read the school's policy on teaching and learning and discuss it with the teacher.		Having observed children, make a list of the opportunities for structured play or exploration.		Plan and teach activities, relating these to theories of learning.	Evaluate the children's learning and use this information to reflect on the suitability of the teaching approach you used.
How do you create a learning environment?		Observe how the teacher manages the movement of children around the classroom.		Audit classroom resources.	Use a variety of strategies for managing transitions with the whole class.	Evaluate the effectiveness of different strategies for transitions.
How do you plan for learning and teaching?	Read NLS and NNS medium-term plans for the period for which you are on placement. Read curriculum policies for any additional subjects you will be teaching.			Plan a sequence of lessons including science and several foundation subjects; produce an overview grid for these subjects. Produce weekly planning based on the NLS and NNS.		Amend your planning after teaching on a daily and weekly basis.
How do you assess and record children's learning?	Find out about the school's policy on assessment and marking.	Observe whether and how teachers involve children in self-assessment.		Plan, organise and lead a self-assessment activity with a small group of children. Plan to use a specific assessment strategy to gather evidence from a group of children or the whole class.		Review children's involvement in self-assessment. Evaluate the assessment strategy you used with the class in terms of the quality of the evidence and information it provided about the children's learning.
One school for all?	Consider the possible effects of race, gender, class, disability and impairment on children.	Carry out an audit of the resources available in the classroom in terms of gender, disability, cultural/ethnic, linguistic and religious diversity.		Plan to improve strategies used in one of the following: interpreting the curriculum; inclusive teaching strategies; behaviour management.	Gather examples of strategies used to ensure equal access to the curriculum.	Evaluate the strategies you are using to ensure equal access to the curriculum.

All the activities in this chapter are outlined in full and have the following information provided with them:

⊃ essential background to the activity including such items as which equipment to use and which setting might be most appropriate for carrying it out;
⊃ a description of the activity and all the elements which go to make it up;
⊃ ideas on how to evaluate its success;
⊃ suggested further, background reading;
⊃ your achievements.

Chapter 4 — How do you define yourself in the role of the teacher?

Link to Professional Standards for QTS

Please refer to the Appendix for information about the links between this theme and the Professional Standards for the Award of Qualified Teacher Status.

Becoming a teacher

A successful teacher could be said to be one who stimulates children's natural curiosity and channels it towards productive ends. This is no mean feat. Achieving this with one child is a challenge, achieving it with 30 individuals at the same time requires a great deal of forethought and detailed planning. One of the most effective methods of engaging a class of children in a learning activity is to create an atmosphere of excitement and enthusiasm. This is mainly achieved through the behaviour of the teacher, providing a role model for the children. There are many parallels between teaching and acting, not least that you are often required to play a part. In the context of the classroom, learning will be given purpose if the children are convinced of its importance by the attitude of the teacher.

The start of every lesson should be confident, reasserting the teacher's status in the classroom. It should also be the start of a 'learning adventure' for every child. When planning a lesson on any subject, the starting point must be something of relevance to children. Planning the initial presentation of the lesson content can make or break the success of a lesson or even an entire topic. Going through the planning process in detail will give any trainee or teacher a feeling of confidence which will be clearly communicated to the children.

Children's lives are affected by many influences outside of school, not least their parents. Changes in legislation mean that parents are entitled to be much more involved and informed about their children's education. This has led schools to formalise many of the procedures surrounding home-school contact. Schools will have written policies and individual teachers will have unwritten but firmly held systems in place for communicating with parents. As a trainee you must follow school policy at all times.

Of course, parents can be enormously supportive of their children's education and a great help in the classroom. Many parents like to be involved in classroom activities such as listening to children read and assisting with practical activities. On these occasions it is important to demonstrate good organisation, confidence and have a precise plan for the role of the parent in the classroom. It is usually best to avoid parents working with their own children and some schools insist on them working in a different class. Taking a professional, straightforward approach will enable you to make the most of such assistance and help the parent feel more involved in school life.

Preparation
Read Hayes (1999) Chapter 3.

Task
Obtain and read the school's policy on parental partnership. Make sure you have a clear understanding of when and how you communicate with parents on a formal basis. Discuss with the teacher the rules and routines which involve parents, such as the beginning and end of the day, working in the classroom and assisting with trips.

Evaluation and follow up

When parents are helping in the classroom make sure you provide them with a clear plan of what is expected of them and the children. Provide them with some means of giving you feedback about individual children's achievements.

Setting targets for your professional development

As a trainee in the classroom your richest source of information and experience is the teacher. Her role is to provide support and assess your progress; a challenging dual responsibility. The relationship between trainee and teacher is key to the success of the experience, just as the relationship between teacher and child is key to learning. Effective communication and the development of a team approach will allow both parties to capitalise on the learning potential of the situation.

Although the teacher monitors your overall progress, the learning process will be much more effective if you take some responsibility for your own learning. Having clear goals for the short, medium and long term will help you to evaluate your achievements and identify manageable targets for the future. These should be explicitly included in weekly and lesson plans (see **page 54**) and your progress monitored in reflective evaluations (see **page 56**). Having a clear picture of achievements to date will encourage you to persevere when you encounter challenges and motivate you to keep striving for improvement. This is something which should continue throughout your teaching career.

Preparation

Read Kyriacou (1991) Chapter 8.

Task

During your discussions with the teacher, set approximately three specific targets for your development for the following week. These should relate closely to the Standards for the Award of Qualified Teacher Status from the TTA (2002). Work on an element of these targets in every lesson. Lesson plans should have a section identifying which target (or part of a target) you are focusing on and evaluations should clearly analyse your progress towards this.

Evaluation and follow up

During a discussion with the teacher, evaluate your progress towards these targets and set new targets for the following week.

Respectful relationships

Knowledge and understanding of children's personalities and learning needs are central to the teacher-pupil relationship. Children respond to the teacher, the learning and each other in many different ways. Each of these relationships contributes to the child's self-esteem, motivation and readiness for learning. Monitoring these aspects can provide the teacher with vital information which can be used to plan appropriate learning experiences. It is important to learn when to listen and watch, rather than intervene, in order to develop a deeper understanding of what motivates children.

In developing an understanding of each child, the teacher can plan the content and styles of learning which will maximise children's potential. Planning should take into account prior learning and levels of understanding. Using questioning techniques which encourage participation by all members of the class and avoiding making assumptions about children's potential levels of achievement will enhance motivation and build children's confidence and self-esteem. This requires careful analysis of children's progress and perceptions – teachers need to be able to focus on what children have learned rather than what they think they have taught. There can actually be a substantial gap between the two! The resulting knowledge can be used to establish realistic but challenging targets for learning and behaviour. Communicating these to the class simply and clearly will increase children's motivation to learn through a collaborative effort towards shared goals.

Learning cannot be detached from the social context of the classroom and children's wider lives. A child's emotional and physical well-being can influence his or her readiness to learn. To address the physical needs of children, schools provide a warm, safe environment, a meal at lunchtime, and some provide breakfast to ensure that all children are ready to start the day. Similarly, the emotional needs of the children must be met before they are ready to learn. As Hayes (1999, page 58) outlines, in order to feel sufficiently confident to contribute their ideas, children must be secure in the knowledge that their input will be respected and received with encouragement. This will enhance their self-esteem and contribute to a positive atmosphere in the classroom.

There will be times when children are deeply affected by emotional upheaval and insecurity outside school: illness, a quarrel with a friend, a family break-up or moving house. At these times it may be necessary to act as counsellor and provide trusted support before you can expect the child to take part in the planned learning. Children can be taught to share problems and support each other. Through techniques such as circle time a non-threatening, compassionate ethos can be created which can be used to dissipate tensions and increase co-operation and self-esteem.

Preparation
Read Fisher (1995) Chapter 9.

Task
Plan and teach a short activity which focuses on building children's self-esteem. It may be a circle time activity with an open discussion and sharing of feelings and ideas. Consider how you will set the tone of the activity and ensure that all children feel confident and able to take part. Make sure that children have plenty of opportunities to express their feelings and ideas and that you respond to them positively.

Evaluation and follow up
Review and evaluate the activity immediately afterwards. Focus on the ways in which the children responded to you and each other. Identify those who took part with confidence and how quieter children reacted to your encouragement. Use this information to continue to plan for building children's self-esteem and motivating them during future lessons. When assessing and monitoring children's progress, take account of these issues.

Successful Communication

Schools are sizeable communities in themselves and as such they need effective communication systems so that every member has the information he or she needs. Some of these relationships are sensitive and communication needs to be personal. Other relationships are public and require information to be disseminated quickly to a large group. These relationships relate to those which occur on a smaller scale in the classroom. In each case finding an appropriate time and place for one-to-one discussion is just as important as making sure that important information is put on a notice board or sent to everyone on paper.

Schools will have formal systems of meetings, appointments, timetables, shared plans, newsletters and parents' evenings. Individual teachers will have their own less formal systems of disseminating information. Registration and home times are often used to communicate important messages to the whole class, teachers may be available to parents before and after school, notes may be written in homework diaries or home/school records, notices may be put on the door or notice board. These systems are many and varied but essential to the efficient running of the class and school. Trainees should become familiar with them as soon as possible and make good use of them when appropriate.

In the classroom, the main form of communication between teacher and children is speech. Through subtle use of the voice, slight alterations in tone, pace, pitch, projection, manner and range, teachers can communicate on many levels. This is all part of the 'performance' teachers put on every day. The teacher's voice can be used to control the mood and atmosphere in the classroom, to convey pleasure or displeasure, to control the noise level or achieve instant quiet and stillness and the full attention of every child. Trainees will need to develop a range of 'voices' and learn when to use them to best effect.

Non-verbal means of communication, which does not interrupt the flow of the lesson, can be equally useful. A stern look is less intrusive than a harsh word but is as clear in its meaning and can be used to reaffirm behavioural expectations. A smile indicates approval and acts as a reward – accompanied by raised eyebrows it can signal the end of a joke and the expectation that work will resume. Gestures and movements can be used in similar ways. A pointed finger accompanied by a smile can single out a child's achievement in a large group.

Preparation
Read Moyles and Robinson (2002) pages 57–62.

Observe the range of communication techniques used by the teacher. It will be useful to divide these techniques into spoken, written and physical forms of communication. In particular, focus on the ways in which the teacher communicates approval and praise to individuals and the whole class. Notice the differences between styles of communication with children, teaching assistants and parents.

Identify the effects of these different forms of communication. Focus on how communication from the teacher affects the children's attitudes and behaviour as well as their learning.

Task
Plan and teach a lesson for a group of children during which you clearly communicate your expectations for learning and behaviour. Provide encouragement and support during the lesson and celebrate the children's achievements at the end, referring back to your original expectations.

Evaluation and follow up
Which children met your expectations? How did the clear communication of expectations affect the children's learning? Identify the ways in which the children responded to your praise. How will you incorporate these strategies into your future teaching?

Your achievements

Now you have read this section and completed the activities you should be able to:

➲ generate enthusiasm for learning by providing an appropriate role model;
➲ recognise the need for schools to have a clear policy on parental partnerships and the need to follow it at all times;
➲ communicate with parents successfully;
➲ include targets for your development in lesson, weekly and medium-term plans;
➲ review your progress regularly with the teacher;
➲ plan for and use a range of teaching styles, responding to the academic, social and emotional needs of the children;
➲ communicate clear expectations of learning and behaviour to the class;
➲ celebrate children's achievements and provide feedback on progress;
➲ evaluate and respond to children's levels of self-esteem;
➲ communicate effectively with individuals, groups and the whole class using verbal and non-verbal means;
➲ observe and categorise forms of communication used by the teacher;
➲ identify some of the effects of this communication on children's learning.

If you feel that you have completed the tasks successfully, return to the relevant needs analysis and mark it off with the date and evidence. Ask your tutor about being able to use this activity as evidence that you have met the Professional Standards for QTS. Refer to the summary of Standards listed in the Appendix.

Chapter 4   How do children learn and teachers teach?

Link to Professional Standards for QTS

Please refer to the Appendix for information about the links between this theme and the Professional Standards for the Award of Qualified Teacher Status.

Theories of learning

Why do we need theories of learning? One reason is that teaching is not something that 'just happens'. The way that you approach teaching will be determined by a number of influences: your personality, your values and fundamental beliefs about teaching and learning, and the range of techniques and strategies you adopt and refine with experience. The way you teach and the strategies you adopt are not just a matter of whim. They should be based on clear evidence of what is effective. The understanding of what is meant by 'effective' in learning and teaching continues to be debated in education and you will begin to recognise the complexity of this debate as you develop as a teacher. This chapter will explore some of the theories which inform our understanding of how children learn and consider the implications of these for teaching.

There have always been theories about how children (or adults) learn. Different cultures have different ideas about the most effective way to learn. The rote learning of the past, for example, is now much less in evidence in the primary classroom, although it may still be useful for some forms of knowledge.

Refining and applying your understanding

You now have an awareness of the major theories of learning which have influenced the development of primary education in Britain and you have begun to observe how these influence learning and teaching in the classroom. You need to refine and apply your understanding to support children in their learning and develop effective teaching approaches.

You will see a range of activities, based on different theoretical approaches, in any classroom. You will be able to identify the theoretical basis of the learning and teaching you see. The following are all based on particular theoretical approaches, which are discussed on **pages 9–11**.

Example: *Patrick is using a computer program in which he has to measure angles with an on-screen protractor. The computer responds to each successful attempt with a reward or corrects any errors. This could be regarded as based on a behaviourist approach to learning, whilst the following are all underpinned by constructivist theories.*

A class of children is divided into groups. Each group plants cress seeds in pots of compost. The plants are left in a variety of different growing conditions for two weeks and the children record and compare the growth of their plants.

Kate in a Key Stage 2 class has created a poster using a desktop publishing program. After saving her work she experiments by changing the colours of the background and the fonts to see which combination she likes best.

In RE, a group of Key Stage 2 children are looking at a range of artefacts, all of which are sources of light. They are researching in books and making drawings and notes about the uses of the artefacts and their symbolic role in the different religious festivals.

Preparation

During your placement, observe the opportunities for structured play or exploration in the curriculum and note:

- ➲ what subjects or areas of learning are involved;
- ➲ what sort of learning this activity is designed to bring about;
- ➲ how the children interact;
- ➲ how adults intervene in this learning.

Task

Plan some teaching for a group or class. How does the planned learning and teaching relate to the learning theories discussed above? Which approaches do you plan to use?

Evaluation and follow up

Look at your lesson evaluations. Were there aspects of the lesson you were not happy with? Did this relate to the teaching approach you adopted? How could another approach have been used? Might it have been more successful?

Responding to children's work

It is important to remember what we understand about children's learning when planning for the classroom. Try also to think of the implications of this when responding to their work, orally or in your written comments. Think in particular about the ways in which you respond in writing. Which of these is most likely to help a child develop?

- ➲ writing 'a lovely piece of writing' at the end of a story; or
- ➲ writing 'a lovely piece of writing – you have made very good use of adjectives to describe the characters'.

It is important that the comments are both appropriate for the age group and provide useful feedback for the child. Further information on marking and responding to children's work is given in the theme on assessing and recording children's learning.

The concept of 'fitness for purpose'

In looking at the use of different teaching strategies you will have realised that you need to base your teaching approach on various factors, particularly on what will best help the children achieve the learning objective. Other factors may influence the choices you make. For example, timetable constraints or the availability of resources may limit the opportunity you have in particular circumstances. However, whatever the circumstances, the methods you adopt must be 'fit for purpose'.

First expressed by Alexander, Rose and Woodhead in their critique of teaching methods published in 1992, the idea of fitness for purpose has become a significant influence on the development of practice in British primary schools. There is no one learning theory or teaching approach which is suitable for every situation. The choice of approach and the learning theory which underpins it must be appropriate to the learning objective, and it must be 'fit for purpose'. You will find the same term used when looking at forms of organisation in the classroom and this is discussed further in the theme on organising the learning environment on **page 79**.

Exploring teaching strategies

A great deal of talking goes on in the classroom. Contrary to what you may think, most of this talking is done by the teacher! For a description of some influential research into classroom talk you may like to read the work of Galton *et al.* (1980) and Tizard and Hughes (1984).

The way in which you communicate with children is based to a great extent on your choice of teaching strategies and you will use a wide range of approaches in the classroom. Each has a particular purpose, needs to be carefully planned and suitable for the learning objective. The terminology used to describe different teaching strategies may vary in the texts you read. Direct teaching based on specific, planned, close interactions between the teacher and the children is generally recognised as having several elements. You may find the following descriptions helpful to clarify your understanding of the key terms.

Explanation

When you are explaining something to children you provide information in a logical, structured sequence. As well as giving information you may also offer examples and give reasons. You will have planned very carefully what you are going to say in your explanation and will have thought through, and may have recorded in your lesson plan, the vocabulary you are going to use. It is particularly important to plan any subject-specific or technical vocabulary which may be new to some or all of the children.

Example: *The teacher explains why it is important that when working on the PE apparatus children take turns in an orderly and quiet manner.*

Example: *In a data handling activity the teacher explains that the children are going to visit other classes and collect information about the hypothesis they are testing. She reminds the children that they are collecting information under various headings and that in information handling these are called 'fields'.*

Exposition

In a way similar to explanation, the children are *exposed* to information but with a greater emphasis on illustration, through examples, objects or pictures.

Example: *A teacher introduces some work on the Victorians by describing vividly how their locality might have looked, and been experienced, by Victorian children of their age.*

In explanation and exposition most, if not all, of the talking is done by the teacher with the children as listeners. However, this is a two-way process and you need to be aware of the responsiveness of the children, their engagement and body language to make sure of their understanding. Always be prepared to adapt or change what you are saying, or the way you are saying it, in the light of the children's responses and attention. Make sure you vary the pace of your exposition, allow time for questions and plan some interesting follow-up activity for the children to do.

Demonstration

The teacher uses a range of resources and equipment to demonstrate particular skills or techniques.

Example: *Children are going to do some observational drawings using a range of pencils. The teacher demonstrates the ways in which pencils of varying hardness can be used for sketching, shading and smudging.*

Modelling

Similar in many ways to demonstrating, a skill, process or technique is modelled by the teacher or by another child, providing an example which can be copied or developed.

Example: *The teacher asks several children to show others the different ways they are able to travel across some PE apparatus.*

Questioning

Teachers are unique as a profession in that they constantly ask questions to which they already know the answer! Effective questioning can be one of the most useful tools in your armoury and a powerful way of developing children's understanding.

Questions can be defined as 'lower order' which are often 'closed' questions to which there is a single answer. 'Higher order' questions tend to be 'open' or probing questions which demand more sophisticated levels of thinking and which invite a number of responses rather than a right or wrong answer. These different types of question have a different purpose in teaching. Closed questions generally test knowledge or understanding, while open or probing questions require analysis, synthesis, evaluation or exploration. Such questions might include the following forms of words:

⊃ What does this picture tell us?
⊃ How could we find out more about …?
⊃ What is your evidence for saying that?
⊃ Can you explain how you worked that out?

There are a number of traps which it is easy to fall into when questioning children:

⊃ Make sure you allow time for children to think and respond. It is easy to become anxious when there seems to be no response to a question and to move on too quickly. Keep your nerve and allow a few moments of silence before trying again! As a practical suggestion, try to allow four seconds' thinking time before moving on.
⊃ If a child gives an incorrect answer, try to use this response to develop understanding. It may be a sensible guess or indicate partial understanding that can be built upon.
⊃ If the answer is incorrect, don't just repeat the question, or worse still, nag or cajole the children for a response. Try to think of a question which calls on them to consider a similar example, or prompt them with something that relates to their current understanding. Use phrases like:
  ⊃ Do you remember when we talked about this yesterday?
  ⊃ What happened when you …?
  ⊃ Can you think of another example similar to this?

Avoid ambiguity in questions, asking several questions together, repeating a question or asking the same question in a different form too soon. However, rephrasing the question can sometimes help children's understanding.

Generally speaking, open questions, which invite the child to explore or reflect, are more productive than closed questions to which there is one correct answer. Overuse of closed questioning may cause frustration or anxiety, or may lead to a game in which children think they have to guess what answer the teacher wants, rather than thinking carefully about their response.

Questions can also be used to probe children's understanding. This particular form of questioning is sometimes referred to as 'elicitation'. It is discussed in greater detail on **page 86**.

Developing your practice

Your practice will be an ongoing cycle in which observation in the classroom will provide you with models to explore and approaches you may wish to try for yourself. Analysing both children's learning and your teaching will enable you to evaluate the effectiveness of the approaches you are using. This process will be informed by ongoing observation as you continue your partnership with your class teacher and the children in your care.

Preparation
Remind yourself of Gardner's multiple intelligences which are described on **pages 12–13**.

Task
Look back through your medium-term and lesson planning. Find examples of activities which correspond to Gardner's multiple intelligences:

	Example one	Example two
Linguistic		
Mathematical and logical		
Visual and spatial		
Musical		
Interpersonal		
Intrapersonal		
Kinaesthetic		

Evaluation and follow up

Reflect on the following questions in your evaluation.

⮕ Is there a good range of different approaches in your planned activities?
⮕ Have you planned to use approaches which correspond to the differing capacities of children in your class?

Think about how you can motivate and challenge children in different ways.

Your achievements

Now you have read this section and completed the activities you should be able to:

⮕ refine and apply your understanding of how children learn to your developing professional practice;
⮕ recognise and provide opportunities for structured play or exploration;
⮕ evaluate children's learning in the light of the teaching approach adopted;
⮕ explore how alternative teaching approaches might be more successful;
⮕ motivate and challenge children by using a range of interesting teaching approaches;
⮕ respond appropriately and helpfully to children's work;
⮕ understand the concept of 'fitness for purpose' as applied to teaching strategies and use this in your own practice;
⮕ explore the use of different teaching approaches such as explanation, exposition and so on;
⮕ understand that different types of questions have different purposes in teaching;
⮕ develop and evaluate your use of different types of questioning in your teaching.

If you feel that you have completed the tasks successfully, return to the relevant needs analysis and mark it off with the date and evidence. Ask your tutor about being able to use this activity as evidence that you have met the Professional Standards for QTS. Refer to the summary of Standards listed in the Appendix.

Chapter 4 How do you create a learning environment?

Link to Professional Standards for QTS

Please refer to the Appendix for information about the links between this theme and the Professional Standards for the Award of Qualified Teacher Status.

Routines and rules

Managing a whole class is similar in many ways to working with a group, but more challenging. The rules and routines you will have used and observed while working with groups will be of great use with the whole class. You may need to be firmer, but this does not mean you will need to adopt a harsh, unfriendly or dictatorial style with the children. Make references to class rules which children have agreed to rather than making personal criticisms of individual children. This will encourage children to develop self-discipline rather than the teacher enforcing good behaviour through fear of humiliation. You must make sure the children are aware of what is expected of them; be explicit in stating your expectations of their behaviour and learning. When working with a group alongside an experienced teacher you will have followed class routines and encouraged children to obey the agreed rules. Now you are managing the whole class and will need to develop your own strategies for maintaining a positive working atmosphere through co-operation and shared responsibility for keeping to the class rules.

Most children will need regular reminders of the rules. These may be given orally and reinforced by a prominent sign on the class notice board. Oral reminders should be predominantly positive, praising children who are following the rules and spreading the rewards amongst the class. Where a negative response is necessary, it should be delivered quietly and calmly, directly to the individual rather than being a public event which distracts others and humiliates the child. Keep reward systems simple and give praise where it is due rather than indiscriminate congratulation, this should avoid children becoming 'praise junkies' and encourage the development of self-discipline.

It is essential to avoid conflict for the safety and security of all members of the class, including those who need serious reminders about their behaviour. Calm reminders of class rules can usually be achieved through the use of simple strategies such as sitting beside a child rather than standing over or sitting opposite them, and lowering your voice rather than raising it. This allows you to be firm without jeopardising your relationships with individual children or interrupting the working atmosphere in the classroom. Safety is paramount and it may occasionally be necessary for a child to leave the class for his or her own safety or that of others. 'Time out' gives the child the opportunity to escape from a difficult situation and usually diffuses tension. In most cases it will need to last for only a few minutes before the child is ready to rejoin the class. It is essential that the child has a safe place to go where he or she is supervised and has something constructive to do.

If children are repeatedly misbehaving and disrupting the learning of others, question yourself as to the cause of this. It may not be a social or behavioural problem but rather a result of inappropriate expectations in relation to work. Children who are well motivated and engaged in learning are much less likely to misbehave or disrupt the class. Tasks should provide a sufficient challenge for children but be within their capabilities. Children who are bored by easy work or demoralised by difficult work are likely to find alternative sources of occupation which may involve attention seeking and disruptive behaviour.

Effective management involves anticipating problem areas and taking preventative action rather than reacting to problems that arise. Making good use of learning support assistants (LSAs) and other adults to monitor children's work and behaviour can be useful. This must be carefully managed and roles and responsibilities agreed in advance. The use of successful strategies during particularly troublesome periods of the day will minimise opportunities for disruption. For example, times when children all need to move from place to another can be problematic.

Preparation
Read Pollard (1997) pages 235–40 and Cowley (2001) Chapter 3 to learn more about transitions in the classroom.

Focus on a short period of movement in the classroom such as the handing in or collection of work, tidying up, going out to break or lining up. Observe the strategies employed by the class teacher which end one activity and move smoothly to the next.

Task
Over a period of several days, develop a successful strategy for stopping the class and quickly getting their attention. Use a variety of techniques to move the children in groups. You might use their working groups, based on how quickly they are ready or how well they have worked. Alternatively use questioning such as 'Who has a birthday in May?' or 'Who is wearing grey socks?', avoiding using criteria relating to sensitive issues such as gender.

Evaluation and follow up
Identify which strategies were most effective and why. Make a list of other techniques that could be used to increase the efficiency of transition periods in the classroom.

Expectations

Clear expectations are vital to the smooth running of the class, but it is essential to recognise that there will be occasions which are not governed by the established rules and exceptions will need to be made. When dealing with a larger number of children, there are more likely to be exceptions. Through your relationship with the class you will develop a good understanding of individuals' behaviour and ability. There will be children who respond quickly to a stern look and those who need stronger and more regular reminders. Knowledge of the reasons for children's behaviour will allow you to make informed judgements about avoiding confrontation. Using established class routines will minimise the distraction inevitably caused by a new adult in the classroom.

You will need to be aware of children who have Individual Education Plans (IEPs) for behaviour and how these children need to be dealt with. Being aware of the emotional and social context of individuals which may affect behaviour in school will also help you to be sensitive whilst maintaining a safe and stimulating working environment. Events such as parental separation, a new baby, moving house, unemployment, family illness and bereavement will all have a significant effect on children's well-being and probably their behaviour in school. They may become withdrawn, lose concentration or demand more attention and will need special sensitivity and care.

Expectations of children's learning may also need to be varied for children with very different needs. Individuals or groups of children who have IEPs may need to have separate learning objectives for some lessons. You will need to consider carefully the way in which these different expectations are communicated to the child or children concerned. They need to know what is expected of them as much as any other child but must not be singled out publicly or highlighted as different.

Preparation
Read Jacques and Hyland (2000) Chapter 13 and MacGrath (2000) pages 69–71.

Task
Focus on a child with Special Educational Needs. Observe a lesson in which the teacher has different expectations of behaviour and/or learning, for example, the behaviour management expectations and

techniques used to facilitate learning for a child with autism, dyspraxia or behavioural difficulties in a mainstream class.

Evaluation and follow up
How are the teacher's expectations signalled to the class/individual? How are the teacher's expectations communicated to an individual child? How is this achieved without disruption to learning? How does this support the child's learning?

Timing

Every lesson that you teach needs variations in pace and activities. This will ensure that children are able to work for extended periods of time and will avoid possible demotivation through tiredness and the monotony of working in a particular way for too long. Ensure that lessons contain quiet periods during which children have the opportunity to think and digest what they have learned. Communicating your enthusiasm, whether real or pretend, will help to motivate children and keep up the pace of the lesson. Do not underestimate the influence of your attitude to the work presented to children. They will pick up on your mood and approach and this will have an enormous effect on their learning. Teaching involves providing a role model for children and this can entail some strategic acting on the part of the teacher, especially when you are teaching a lesson about which you are unsure or uninspired.

When you are teaching a whole class it is important to evaluate the lesson as it progresses, monitoring children's learning and motivation. You will develop the ability to make changes as you are working. This may mean changing or even abandoning the lesson you are teaching if it is failing to inspire children sufficiently for them to meet the learning objectives. It is important to judge when to do this, before children begin to feel that they are failing, thereby undermining their confidence. You will need to develop a repertoire of short activities and techniques to use in such situations. Ideally these should be adaptable for use in a variety of curriculum subjects and should develop children's problem-solving and thinking skills. The classroom needs to be organised in such a way that it is easy to move from one activity to another without disruption and that alternative resources are easily accessible if necessary.

Preparation
Read Hayes (1999) pages 86–92.

Task
In order to research ideas for short lessons, discuss short lessons with other teachers in the school. Ask each one for some suggestions for purposeful short activities to use with the whole class. Make a list and keep it in the classroom, ensuring that any resources needed are listed and readily available.

Communication

Good teaching is based on positive relationships with children. Good relationships have their foundations in successful communication. There are many ways of keeping children well informed about expectations and learning, the importance of which is outlined above. Much information must be explicitly given to children, but notice boards and signs can be used to remind and update. The younger the children, the more important spoken and non-verbal information becomes. Physical communication, such as how you stand or sit when teaching or talking to children, is just as important as what you say. Children need to feel included and accepted in order to develop confidence and security in the learning environment. However large your class is, make an effort to ensure you have a conversation with every child every day. In order to preserve a secure learning environment, ensure that the majority of interactions are positive and open.

This atmosphere of openness and clear communication should also be applied to your relationships with other members of staff and other adults who work within the school. In particular, make sure you liaise with year group colleagues and subject leaders to organise cross-class aspects such as shared resources, access to shared areas, planning and working with children in ability sets. You will also need to work

closely with LSAs and parent helpers who work with children in your class. T[
have very different roles, working with groups, individuals or providing gen[
support, and these must be made clear to make best use of this vital resource

Preparation
Read Moyles and Robinson (2002) pages 44–45 and MacGrath (2000) pages 72–8.

Observe the ways in which the teacher makes use of LSAs during lessons. Note whether they work with groups or individuals and the ways in which they support children's learning.

Task
Plan and teach a lesson in which an LSA works with a group of children. Make sure you provide guidance on your expectations and opportunities to discuss children's progress and misconceptions.

Evaluation and follow up
Record information about children's learning from the LSA. Identify the ways in which the LSA supported children's learning and the ways in which you could have made better use of his or her time.

Managing children

Children operate as individuals and members of groups, the class and the school. Organising them for learning requires a sensitive and flexible approach. The way they are organised needs to suit the activity, teaching and learning style. This is known as fitness for purpose. If children are to be paired or grouped, consider whether this is done according to ability, friendship, gender or personality, or indeed a mixture of these. If children usually work in particular groupings, changing these tends to cause disruption; however, confident, independent learners will be capable of coping with this and all children should be encouraged to work in a variety of ways. Different groupings may be used within a lesson. For example the literacy hour utilises whole class, group and individual work and requires careful consideration and organisation of the children for the different sections of the lesson. Children may need to use the space in the classroom in different ways according to how they are organised.

Certain points in the day are pivotal. They set the tone for the day or the next lesson and provide opportunities for informal communication and pastoral activities. These are usually periods where the whole class comes together for a short time, often on the carpet area. The importance of this time should not be underestimated, for older children as well as for those in Key Stage 1 and the foundation stage. It can be a time for celebrating individual and group achievements and reinforcing a positive atmosphere in the classroom. These periods need to be managed sensitively in order to maintain an open, calm mood and ensure all children feel secure and involved.

The start of the morning or afternoon and the end of the day provide opportunities for both personal interactions with children and preparation for and consolidation of learning. Taking the register, reading a story or organising 'show and tell' sessions can provide occasions to have informal discussions with children which can help to establish positive personal relationships with individuals. Both teacher and children should find this time enjoyable and productive.

Preparation
Read Hayes (1999) pages 117–19 and Kyriacou (1991) pages 41–3.

Observe a lesson focusing on the way the children are grouped and organised throughout.

- ➲ What forms of grouping are used?
- ➲ What types of groupings have been used?
- ➲ How have the children been encouraged to work collaboratively?
- ➲ How do these groupings change to suit different teaching and learning styles?
- ➲ How is the classroom organised to facilitate different groupings?

- How are adults used to support learning?
- What are the advantages and disadvantages of whole class work?
- What are the advantages and disadvantages of group work?
- What are the advantages and disadvantages of individual work?

Task
Work with several groups of children grouped in a variety of ways throughout the week. Take account of the grouping in your planning.

Evaluation and follow up
Identify the ways in which different groupings affect individuals' learning in positive and negative ways.

Resources

You are now planning and teaching whole class lessons. Lesson plans should include an itemised list of the resources needed for each lesson. Part of your preparation for lessons will be ensuring that appropriate resources are available and in good working order. This should be done as early as possible before the lesson, with some resources needing to be ordered or organised several days or weeks before the lesson takes place. This level of preparation is necessary in order to encourage independent learning and to avoid disrupting learning. As you take more responsibility for classroom organisation and whole class work, you will need to ensure that consumable resources are replaced when necessary. Equipment shared with other classes will need to be carefully looked after and maintained.

Of course the classroom itself is an important learning resource and the organisation of furniture and display space should best facilitate the planned learning. It is ideal to arrange the classroom in such a way that it is flexible enough to be used for a variety of lessons and learning styles without frequent reorganisation. Similarly, displays should be created that will support and enhance learning for several weeks. Some displays should celebrate children's achievements and learning, others should be more interactive, including investigative equipment, questions, challenges and books as well as posters and children's work.

Preparation
Read Moyles (1992) Chapter 2.

Task
Carry out a resource audit of your classroom. This will familiarise you with the resources that are available. Using medium-term plans for the next half term, make a list of resources that you will need to organise in advance and people you will need to speak to. Investigate what is available in school, taking advice from subject leaders and colleagues.

Your achievements

Now you have read this section and completed the activities you should be able to:

- apply established classroom routines and rules to management of the whole class;
- plan and teach whole class lessons;
- recognise a variety of reasons for children's misbehaviour;
- make effective use of other adults in the classroom;
- use a range of strategies to organise transition periods between activities;
- stop the class and gain their attention quickly;
- be aware of the need to vary expectations and teaching techniques to meet the varying needs of the children in the class;
- recognise the need for varied activities during the day;
- provide purposeful activities for children when lessons are cut short;
- communicate effectively with children and adults in the classroom;
- plan for the use of LSAs in lessons;
- gather useful information from LSAs about the achievements of individuals;
- evaluate the effectiveness of your use of LSAs to support children's learning;
- match the organisation of children to the activity and learning objective;

● make good use of whole class time to maximise communication and build positive relationships with the children;
● identify and organise the resources needed for a lesson;
● carry out a resource audit of the classroom.

If you feel that you have completed the tasks successfully, return to the relevant needs analysis and mark it off with the date and evidence. Ask your tutor about being able to use this activity as evidence that you have met the Professional Standards for QTS. Refer to the summary of Standards listed in the Appendix.

Link to Professional Standards for QTS

Please refer to the Appendix for information about the links between this theme and the Professional Standards for the Award of Qualified Teacher Status.

Planning for the class

You have already planned for the work of a group, planning your lessons with specific learning objectives, and using your evaluations of children's learning and of your teaching to refine and develop your planning. Now you are ready to develop your planning and teaching skills, taking on greater responsibility for the work of the class as a whole and for a wider range of subjects. You will probably still be working from the teacher's medium-term planning, although you may have the opportunity to participate in the medium-term planning process, depending on the timing of your school experience placement. However, you will have responsibility for preparing weekly planning and individual lesson plans. Weekly plans in literacy and numeracy will set out the content of these lessons. Further detail about resources, vocabulary, differentiation and organisation will be included in individual lesson plans.

When working with the whole class it is important that you ensure that your formative assessment informs your planning. Knowledge of what the children already know, or can do, is vital if you are to plan lessons that challenge and motivate them. It is relatively easy to evaluate whether the children in a small group have met the learning objective. When working with a whole class you will have to plan formative assessment very carefully to ensure that it provides the information you need to plan your lessons whilst remaining manageable. In this respect, the emphasis on assessment for learning which is developed on **pages 25 and 28** is important.

You should make use of the full range of available documentation: National Curriculum, National Literacy Strategy, National Numeracy Strategy, Curriculum Guidance for the Foundation Stage, school and QCA Schemes of Work, as appropriate, to support your planning.

When you are planning for the whole class you will have to consider whether all the children will complete the same activity or whether you will have several different activities going on at the same time. This will probably vary from one lesson to another. In some lessons all of the children will complete the same activity, in others different activities will be more appropriate. The key issues here are the need to differentiate and that of manageability, both of which may be influenced by the availability of adult support in the classroom.

Example: *In Year 5 the children have been working in groups researching Tudor costume. In ICT they have also taken photographs of themselves using digital cameras. Using their photos opened in a painting package and their knowledge of Tudor costume, they are now producing pictures of themselves as children from Tudor times. All of the children are completing the same activity, although the outcome will differ.*

In a Year 3 mathematics lesson the children have been working on mass. After an introduction to the whole class, they split into four groups, with different activities. Some children have a practical activity with a worksheet to complete, two groups have an investigation based on the weight of coins, while the remaining group works with a learning support assistant on estimating and measuring the mass of some objects in the classroom.

In planning these lessons the teachers have adopted different strategies both in terms of organisation and differentiation. In the first, the differentiation is by outcome and the children will all work on the same task at their own level. In the mathematics lesson the differentiation is by task, with tasks of varying difficulty. There is also differentiation by process as some of the children have the support of a learning assistant.

Bear in mind that when you are planning teaching and learning there are various factors which must be considered. This could include a variety of learning styles or preferred sensory styles (which are discussed in more detail on **pages 103–104**). Other factors include the needs of children who may have English as an additional language, children with special needs and the availability of other adult support in the classroom.

Preparation and task

Working with the teacher's medium-term planning, plan a sequence of lessons in science and several of the foundation subjects. This sequence of lessons should be sufficient to cover all of the work in these subjects over a six-week period. First read the school's curriculum policies and also refer to the other documents available to you such as the school's own curriculum documents, commercial or QCA documents as a source of ideas. Set out your planning in the following format, showing links with the National Curriculum:

Topic:					
	Science	e.g. Art	e.g. History	e.g. Geography	e.g. Music
Week one					
Week two					
Week three					
Week four					
Week five					
Week six					

Write out lesson plans for the first week's lessons, using the format described on **pages 54–55**.

Evaluation and follow up

At the end of the week, based on your evaluations, amend your plan to take account of any necessary changes.

Using ICT for planning

As you will have realised, planning is a time-consuming process. Effective use of ICT, if available, may save you time in setting out your lesson plans, weekly plans and medium-term planning. Once you have a format for your lesson plans which works for you, create an outline or template and save it. You can then re-use this for each of the lessons you need to plan. The same can be done for medium-term planning outlines. All of the National Curriculum and QCA documentation is available online, so you can cut and paste from these documents into your own planning, saving time on writing out or typing from programmes of study or schemes of work. A number of other templates are available for planning. You may wish to consider using some of them, such as those produced by The Skills Factory, which are available on the Internet. The address for these resources is given in the Bibliography.

Planning for literacy and numeracy

Planning for literacy and numeracy is generally undertaken in greater detail than other planning, following guidance issued as part of the national strategies. Although not statutory, these strategies are widely used in schools to plan daily lessons in English and mathematics.

Both the National Literacy and Numeracy Strategies require three levels of planning. In literacy the framework outlines the content to be covered over the long term. Medium-term planning is set out over a period of a half term, with weekly planning which sets out the content and sequence of the literacy hour each day. Experienced teachers may teach from this short-term planning. As a developing practitioner you will probably need to produce individual lesson plans for each of these lessons.

In mathematics, the teaching content is also set out in yearly programmes, with accompanying planning grids. The long-term planning reflects the content of the framework. Medium-term plans are expressed as termly outlines of units of work, with timescales and main teaching objectives identified. Short-term plans set out in detail between five and ten lessons which are taught over a week or fortnight, but again you will need individual lesson plans for each day.

Preparation
Look through the teacher's medium-term planning in literacy and numeracy.

Task
From the medium-term planning in literacy or numeracy, select a week that you are going to plan in detail. Look through the appropriate national strategy to make sure that you are familiar with the material to be taught. Using the outlines suggested in the strategies, or the version of it in use in your school, plan a sequence of five lessons. These must have learning objectives, whole class and differentiated group tasks and plans for a plenary session. Show the planning to your class teacher and discuss it with him or her.

You do not have to teach all of these lessons yourself – your class teacher may wish to share the teaching with you, either within lessons or by covering some of the lessons entirely. However, it is important that you go through the planning process.

Evaluation and follow up
Evaluate each lesson and amend the next day's planning if you need to, based on your formative assessment of the children's attainment. At the end of the week, take some time to review carefully what the children have learned. Record on the planning sheet which children have not achieved the learning objectives for the week as well as those who may have exceeded them. This will then be a record of what the children have learned.

Your achievements

Now you have read this section and completed the activities you should be able to:

➲ develop your skills in planning and take on greater responsibility for planning for the whole class;
➲ plan a sequence of lessons in a range of subjects;
➲ ensure that your planning supports children's learning in a coherent and progressive manner over several weeks;
➲ produce an overview grid to show planned work over several weeks;
➲ undertake detailed weekly planning in literacy and numeracy;
➲ ensure that you assess children and that this formative assessment informs your future planning;
➲ ensure that your planning is compatible with the school's curriculum policies in different subjects;
➲ use a range of documentation to inform your planning, including national strategies and school, QCA or commercial Schemes of Work or Curriculum Guidance for the Foundation Stage as appropriate;
➲ plan differentiated tasks to meet the needs of the range of children in the class;
➲ be aware of children's different learning styles when planning and plan a range of activities to address these different styles;
➲ evaluate and amend your planning, based on your ongoing assessment of children's learning.

If you feel that you have completed the tasks successfully, return to the relevant needs analysis and mark it off with the date and evidence. Ask your tutor about being able to use this activity as evidence that you have met the Professional Standards for QTS. Refer to the summary of Standards listed in the Appendix.

Chapter 4   How do you assess and record children's learning?

Link to Professional Standards for QTS

Please refer to the Appendix for information about the links between this theme and the Professional Standards for the Award of Qualified Teacher Status.

Essential information

The focus of your work at this level will be on extending the range of assessment techniques that you use across a class while trying to keep this manageable. You have previously explored and practised how to observe, listen to and question children. It is essential that you decide who will be assessed, how and when, at the same time as you do your lesson planning.

Consider how other adults can be involved in this assessment process if they are working in the classroom alongside you. Say to yourself, 'what I will be looking for is children who can ...', then address the following questions taken from Fisher (2002, page 190).

Who will gather the evidence, where and when?
Who? (adults)

- the teacher;
- another adult.

With whom? (the children)

- child alone;
- children together;
- children working with the teacher;
- children working with another adult;
- children working without an adult.

Where?

- inside the classroom;
- outside the classroom;
- in the hall;
- in the playground.

When?

- before or after teaching;
- while working with the child/children;
- while child/children are working independently.

Next you need to consider which is the most appropriate assessment technique to use to gather the evidence which you need. It is also important to bear in mind at this stage how this evidence will be recorded. There are some useful guides/pro formas on this available from Mitchell and Koshy (1993) as well as others. The NNS provides an example of a feedback sheet to be used by other adults when working with and assessing the children, which can be modified and adapted according to your needs and is available in the training materials sent to schools.

Developing your proficiency in using a range of assessment techniques

Elicitation

Elicitation is the term given to the process of exploring through discussion of children's ideas and understanding. This is carried out in order to then plan activities which challenge, modify or develop their thinking. There is a move towards recognising that, in certain subject areas such as mathematics and science, research seems to indicate that children at various stages of their development have predictable or anticipated misconceptions. Elicitation can therefore be used to explore these and teaching plans should include questions or activities which challenge these. The following statements elicited from some very young children in science reveal valuable insights into their thinking about the sun and the moon.

'The sun sleeps outside at night, and the moon goes to sleep at the bottom of the sky under a blue cover.' (Aged 4 and 5 months)

'The sun is quite far away, it's by the clouds and near God and when it's night God sleeps on the clouds.' (Aged 4 and 1 month)

Conferencing

This takes the form of an extended discussion between a teacher and an individual child (or sometimes a small group of children). During these discussions it is important to allow a dialogue and seek the child's views on their work, progress and feelings about what they are doing, as well as providing feedback to them based on your own views. It is always helpful to have a few examples of their work which you and/or they have chosen to focus on during the discussion. These discussions are often used to review a child's individual targets and negotiate new targets with them.

Analysing written work and marking

Marking children's work is a common way for teachers to monitor children's learning. Comments from the teacher can be verbal or written depending on the nature of the work and the age of the children. Generally if you are marking young children's work it is a good idea to do this with them so that you can ask questions and explore further what they were thinking or doing. For older children, marking is often something that a teacher takes home to do and so cannot be anything other than an evaluative judgement based on the written evidence alone. Even then, however, it is good practice to engage in a written dialogue with the child and seek clarification of what they were intending, if this is necessary. As discussed earlier, written comments should always refer to what the child has already achieved and then indicate how they might improve this next time or what they need to focus on in the next piece of work. The marking process and the comments you make should be indicative of progress or a sequence of work that the child has been doing.

Example: *It is so good to see how neat your handwriting is today. I can tell you have remembered that all 'tall' (or ascending) letters need to be the same size, which is such an improvement on your last piece of writing. Now you are ready to concentrate on joining up your letters.*

Concept mapping

Concept maps can be used with the whole class at the beginning or end of a unit of work to find out what they know about and how they can connect the different aspects of what they have been studying. They are quite commonly used in mathematics or science where it is important for children to make connections and fit their learning together. Concept maps can also be used with individuals and/or pairs of children. Children might represent these maps in different ways, using a spider diagram, web or even a flow chart to link their ideas, knowledge, vocabulary and so on. The power of concept maps is the opportunity to make explicit the links between these different elements of a topic and their learning or understanding. For further reading on this, refer to Novak and Godwin (1984).

Example: *A Year 5/6 class may be asked to produce a concept map on fractions, decimals and percentages or on the topic of earth and beyond. (See Fig. 4.1.)*

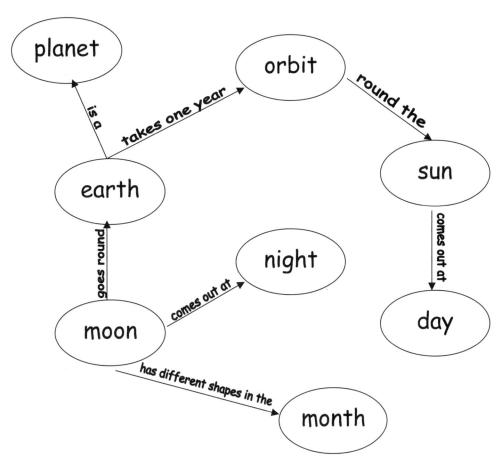

Fig. 4.1   Concept map on the 'earth and beyond' (based on Concept Map in *Primary Science Review* **34**, October 1994).

Planning and evaluating set tasks

One of the greatest challenges to teachers is how to differentiate appropriately. That is how to ensure that children are being challenged at the correct level but not being given work that is too hard or too easy. This also needs to be manageable but meet the needs of the individuals in your class. The National Numeracy and Literacy Strategies have concentrated particularly on offering teachers strategies to ensure that the children are working on the same key objective or theme but this objective can be simplified or extended for different children in the class. The crucial idea is that the children are working on the same idea or concept but usually at three levels of attainment. This might need further adaptation to ensure that all children can be included appropriately (for further details about this refer to the section on 'One school for all', **pages 92–93**). Assessment should be used to monitor and evaluate that these levels of differentiation are working effectively for all children and if not the teacher needs to consider why not and how they might achieve this more successfully.

All the above strategies are used for formative assessment. However, it might be appropriate for you to use a test to assess your class or individuals at this stage in your development, which is a form of summative assessment.

Setting tests
You can devise your own tests on a regular basis such as spelling and tables tests. When doing so always consider the messages you are conveying to children about 'who is good at what' when you read out different lists of words or tables for different groups in the class. Make sure that you have created an ethos in the classroom which celebrates diversity and does not allow children to judge one another or feel humiliated in any way. Be very careful also about who is doing the marking for these tests and whether the results will be publicly announced or kept between you and individual children. Once again, these tests can be sources of anxiety or embarrassment for some children.

You may also set other kinds of tests at the end of a unit of work in a particular subject area, as a way of checking how much the children know or can remember. Recognise the strengths and limitations of these tests. Also, consider assumptions about the nature of learning that underlie them. They are easy to devise, administer and mark but allow you only limited information about the children's actual understanding.

Finally, it is possible to use published tests which allow you to compare the performance of individual children against 'a norm'. These are frequently used to provide reading or spelling ages for children. They can also be used to carry out more careful diagnosis of the needs of children who are causing you concern. There are also optional SATs tests available now for Years 3, 4 and 5 which can be used to provide evidence of performance against the National Curriculum level descriptors.

Why keep records?

Formative records need to be kept in order to provide ongoing information about a child's progress and attainment. Having this information easily available should ensure that teachers take account of it when planning and therefore devise appropriately differentiated activities which will meet the learning needs of the children in the class. These records need to cover all aspects of the child's learning and development (including personal, social and emotional information). However, they may also include contributions from the child, parents or carers as well as other adults who work with the child. It is good practice to make a note of interesting things which the children say and do as part of this data gathering process. These records will also provide an invaluable amount of detail of progress which can be shared with the child, parents or carers at parents' evenings or during informal discussions. However, there is no point in keeping any of this information if it does not directly inform future planning.

Summative records have a different purpose and audience. Since, by definition, they summarise achievement, they need to be relatively short, well focused and organised. As well as noting achievements against key objectives they should contain the most important information about what the child knows, understands and can do. They are often used to pass information on to other teachers, parents, professionals and other schools if the child transfers. Parents are legally entitled to receive an annual report. If it is relevant, this will contain information about their child's performance in the National Curriculum, including the level of their attainment. Feedback from baseline assessment should also be passed on to parents, although this is usually discussed during the first parents' meeting in the autumn term.

Preparation
Read the school policy on assessment and marking. If there is a marking policy, ensure that you adhere to this. Discuss with your teacher whether and how they involve children in self-assessment and observe this, if possible.

Task
Consider how you might involve a small group of children in some self-assessment. Build this into your planning and make clear to the children what you want them to think about.

How are you going to organise, manage and lead this? Will you provide a model to the children of what you want them to consider or have this as a more open discussion? How will you ensure that each individual contributes to and gains from this process? Will the self-assessment focus on one activity or on a more general aspect of their learning? Keep a record of this process.

Evaluation and follow up
What have you learned about encouraging children to reflect on their own progress and how you can facilitate this? What might you consider integrating into your practice in relation to self-assessment on a more regular basis?

Preparation

Decide which of the assessment strategies introduced in this section you can use to gather assessment evidence on a group of children or the whole class for a specific curriculum subject.

Task

Having chosen the curriculum subject you then need to ensure that in planning this assessment task you have addressed a number of questions and issues which will help you gather specific and relevant information about the children's learning. You may wish to record this information on a pro forma or just keep a record of it in a manner which suits you.

- ➲ What am I trying to find out through this assessment?
- ➲ What specific learning am I focusing on?
- ➲ I will be looking for children who can …
- ➲ Who am I going to assess?
- ➲ With whom will they be working?
- ➲ Where will they be working?
- ➲ When will the assessment take place?
- ➲ What assessment strategy will I be using to gather this information?
- ➲ Why have you chosen this strategy?
- ➲ What are the strengths and limitations of this strategy?
- ➲ How will I keep a record of this information?

Evaluation and follow up

The next crucial stage in the process is to consider what you have learned about the children's learning from the evidence you have gathered and how you can use this to inform your future planning and work with them. Consider the following list of questions.

- ➲ Did you find out what you needed to?
- ➲ If not, why not?
- ➲ Could or should you have used a different assessment strategy?
- ➲ How do you think the children felt about the process?
- ➲ Was the recording mechanism you chose suitable and manageable?
- ➲ Were there any surprises in the evidence you collected for individuals/groups/class?
- ➲ What have you discovered about the children's learning that you can use directly to inform your future teaching of them?

Discuss your current understanding of assessment and recording with your teacher and ensure that you are planning and using a variety of strategies to collect information about children's learning. Remember that this must be used to directly inform your teaching.

Your achievements

Now you have read this section and completed the activities you should be able to:

➲ recognise the need to identify at the stage of planning who will be assessing children, where and when;
➲ understand and use a range of assessment strategies including elicitation, conferencing, analysing written work, marking, concept mapping, planning and evaluating set tasks and setting tests;
➲ understand the need for different types of records to be kept related to children's attainment;
➲ be familiar with the school assessment and marking policy and implement this accordingly;
➲ involve children in self assessment, evaluate the success of this process and consider how you will integrate this into your practice;
➲ select and use appropriate assessment strategies with a whole class;
➲ evaluate different assessment strategies and ways of recording this information in your teaching.

If you feel that you have completed the tasks successfully, return to the relevant needs analysis and mark it off with the date and evidence. Ask your tutor about being able to use this activity as evidence that you have met the Professional Standards for QTS. Refer to the summary of Standards listed in the Appendix.

Link to Professional Standards for QTS

Please refer to the Appendix for information about the links between this theme and the Professional Standards for the Award of Qualified Teacher Status.

Essential information

It is essential that you carefully consider the issues related to inclusion in your own class since these are now specifically incorporated into the revised National Curriculum within the three principles listed on **page 30**:

➲ setting suitable learning challenges;
➲ responding to pupils' diverse needs;
➲ overcoming potential barriers to learning and assessment for individuals and groups of pupils.

Inclusion should be seen as an extension of a school's equal opportunities practice and it is important that you are familiar with and adhere to the relevant school policies in the context in which you are currently working.

Before considering the practical elements of inclusion it is worth pausing to consider 'why should we be concerned about issues of race, class, gender, disability and impairment?'.

Preparation and task
Write down some notes on how you would answer this question, before continuing with this section.

Evaluation and follow up
Consider the possible effects of these issues on children.

There are a number of reasons why all teachers should be concerned with and taking a pro-active approach to these issues in order that all children can achieve and these will each be discussed briefly.

Patterns of achievement

There are clear patterns of achievement and underachievement associated with different groups, making these issues an important professional concern. This view is supported by a variety of evidence.

'African-Caribbean, Pakistani and Bangladeshi pupils are markedly less likely to attain five higher grade GCSEs than their White and Indian peers nationally.'
(Gilborn and Mirza 2000 page 12)

'Although at the national level Pakistani youth are less likely to attain five higher grade GCSEs than their white peers, this pattern is reversed in some areas. In four out of ten LEAs that monitor by ethnic origin, Pakistani pupils are more likely to attain this benchmark than white pupils locally.'
(Gilborn and Mirza 2000 page 10)

'Since the late 1980s the attainment gap between the highest and lowest social classes has widened.'
(Gilborn and Mirza 2000 page 18, taken from DFEE data 1999)

'In each of the principal ethnic groups nationally, girls are more likely to achieve five higher grade GCSEs than boys of the same ethnic origin.'
(Gilborn and Gipps 1996 page 24)

Recent data from the Commission for Racial Equality presents final information about permanent exclusions from primary, secondary and special schools in England in the school year 1999/2000 and shows that:

⊃ 84% of permanent exclusions were of boys in 1999/00;
⊃ the rate of exclusion for all black pupils was three times that for all other pupils in 1999/00;
⊃ the permanent exclusion rate for pupils with statements of SEN was seven times as high as that for pupils without statements in 1999/00.

'African-Caribbean pupils are over 4–6 times more likely to be excluded than white pupils although they are no more likely to truant than others. Many of them are children of higher than average ability, although schools see them as underachieving.'
(CRE 2002)

Gypsy traveller children have been identified in an OFSTED report as the most at risk in the education system (in Raising the Attainment of Minority Ethnic Pupils 1999 paragraph 8 page 7). All of this evidence indicates that issues to do with gender, language, race and SEN can impact directly upon educational achievement for individual children.

Equality of opportunity

There are important issues of social justice and human rights here. The National Curriculum (2000) makes very clear the values and purposes underpinning the school curriculum. One of these refers directly to education being one of the routes to 'equality of opportunity for all'.

You might well need to carry out some additional reading at this point if you are not familiar with this area of research or thinking. Refer to the Bibliography on **page 125** for the following in particular:

⊃ Cox, T (ed.) (2000) *Combating Educational Disadvantage*.
⊃ Cole, M (ed.) (1999) *Human Rights, Education and Equality*.
⊃ Hill, D and Cole, M (eds) (2001) *Schooling and Equality: Fact, Concept and Policy*.

Some people may think of Britain as an affluent country where poverty is not an issue of concern today. However, the evidence once again contradicts this perception. Walker and Walker (1997) report that the number of people in Britain living in poverty (which is defined as 50% of average national earnings or less) has increased three fold since 1977 and stood at one quarter of the population in 1997 (cited in Cox, T. (ed) 2000).

Citizenship education
As a teacher, you will be educating children to be citizens of a culturally diverse, democratic society which values everybody and accords them equal rights. You hope they will play a full part in this society. Once again, the National Curriculum (2000) refers to the need for children to develop the ability to value themselves, their families and other relationships, as well as the diversity in society and the environment in which they live. All teachers would aspire to offer a curriculum and use teaching styles and strategies which have these values central to them and as an outcome for all the children with whom they work. However, the reality of many children's experiences of their time in school does not always sit comfortably with these values.

What do we mean by equal opportunities?
Equal opportunities is a very complex issue. It relates to access to:

⊃ the curriculum;
⊃ teacher time;
⊃ resources;
⊃ role models;
⊃ support.

Relationships:

- ➲ between children;
- ➲ between children and staff;
- ➲ with the community.

It is about how teachers raise the awareness and sensitivity of pupils to encourage them to grow up without prejudice. (Hodgetts, 1996)

How can you ensure equal access and opportunities?

There are a number of issues that you need to consider, directly related to your skills and attitudes, when attempting to answer this question. These provide the foundations upon which to build your practice. You will need to recognise that your behaviour is a role model for the children you work with in your class.

Facing the challenge

You may like to consider the following aspects when facing the challenge of adopting a fully inclusive approach.

Creating an appropriate culture in the classroom

From the outset, you will need to establish clear rules, routines and expectations within your classroom for the way children speak, behave and respond to one another. A variety of strategies to achieve this has already been explored in the section on creating and managing the learning environment. An appropriate classroom ethos would be one in which stereotypical views are challenged and pupils learn to view 'differences' between their peers as a positive issue. You will also need explicit procedures for dealing with teasing, bullying or harassment of any kind. In most schools these will be evident in the school policy but you will also need to be confident and comfortable with using these in your classroom and more generally around the school.

Interpreting the curriculum

When planning, ensure that you create and maximise opportunities which recognise and demonstrate respect for pupils' cultural, ethnic, religious and linguistic identities, and actively use these experiences in the classroom.

Curriculum 2000 requires schools to offer a broad and balanced curriculum for all pupils. However, this is only the starting point for planning and you will need to plan your teaching so that it meets and takes account of the needs of individuals and groups of children within your class. It is sometimes beneficial to adopt a thematic approach which makes relevant links between different curriculum areas. This enables children to relate their own experiences of life and the world to the issues they are learning about. In other words, it helps them make a variety of connections within and between subject areas, between their own and other children's experiences and so on. It is also helpful to carefully consider the contexts for learning and ensure that these take account of children's interests and motivation. It is essential to motivate and excite children by planning appropriate work and tasks.

Example: *Use a love of animals or an interest in football to make a book with a child who is a reluctant reader. This can be shared with the class as well, celebrated as an achievement and then used as the child's reading book to encourage them to read more.*

Interpreting the curriculum flexibly is another important aspect of inclusion. The curriculum and the learning opportunities provided should ensure that all children can learn at the appropriate level and experience success. In order to achieve this you might need to make some modifications to the curriculum for individual children or groups of them. The National Numeracy Strategy and the National Literacy Strategy both make recommendations about how to select relevant learning objectives for children across an attainment range.

Example: *Rahela has very good mathematical understanding but a limited vocabulary since English is not her first language. The teacher does not reduce her expectations or limit her mathematical opportunities. Instead, she uses a range of multi-sensory teaching strategies. This means that she provides Rahela with visual clues, models with supportive resources such as 100 squares, points out the link between the spoken language and the relevant mathematical symbols as well as encouraging her to discuss the task with a classroom assistant who also speaks Punjabi.*

Employing inclusive teaching strategies

For teaching strategies to be inclusive they must take account of children's different learning styles. The teacher must also make the decision about which is the most appropriate teaching style to use for the particular task in hand. These issues are discussed in more detail in the section on 'How do children learn and teachers teach?'. There are a number of other issues that need to be taken into account if the teacher is to ensure that barriers to learning are minimised and success in learning maximised for all children.

These involve:

➲ the use of peers as tutors or to support one another;
➲ the supportive role of classroom assistants for individuals or groups;
➲ how technology can be used effectively to support and extend children's learning.

Example: *Two children from different attainment groups may be asked to work together on the computer (one of them with poor writing skills but excellent imagination and oral vocabulary). One of them will be acting as the 'scribe' or doing the typing while they work together to write a poem.*

Assessment plays a crucial role in ensuring that the learning objectives and tasks are appropriate for individuals and groups of children. In this way a teacher can plan manageable differentiation, maintain high expectations for all pupils and use assessment information to inform planning and future teaching. This ongoing monitoring and tracking of individuals' progress is very important if teachers are to critically evaluate the success of the teaching strategies that they are employing. In this way, the children's learning is seen as an indicator of success and allows the teacher to monitor whether they are employing inclusive teaching strategies since these should result in successful progress for all the children in the class.

Many schools are now using sophisticated target-setting systems which allow them to track the progress of individuals, classes and year groups. This data can then be used to monitor achievement and might identify shortcomings or areas of weakness in provision. It could also highlight concerns related to gender or ethnicity within the school if certain groups of children are not making appropriate progress. It would then be important for the school and the teachers to target and address specific areas for attention within their teaching and the curriculum being offered.

Example: *The assessment and monitoring of a particular class might indicate that the boys generally have a much more limited range of spelling strategies. An appropriate response to this information might be to adapt the teaching approaches to include more active games to develop spelling.*

The appropriate organisation and management of the physical environment of the classroom and school will also have to be considered and monitored. This has been discussed in the section on 'creating a learning environment' (see **pages 14–18**).

For further reading see the report by Blair and Bourne (1998) which is in the Bibliography.

Evaluating resources

All resources used in the classroom or the school need to be evaluated to ensure there is no evidence of stereotypes. It is also important to consider whether the materials being used offer positive images of disability, gender and culture. For example, how many books focus on a successful black female or have as their central character a disabled heroine or hero? The Letterbox Library is a very useful source of books which have been carefully selected for use with children. However, all classrooms should also contain, and use on an everyday basis, a wide range of resources (home corner resources, other classroom equipment, artefacts, games, ICT software) which represent different cultural, linguistic and religious identities. Many LEAs have a resource centre which will be able to offer help, guidance and possibly loan items to support your teaching. Parents and members of the community can also be a valuable source of expertise and their involvement will reflect the principle of an inclusive community, of which the school is a part.

Considering behaviour management

A genuinely inclusive teacher would be concerned and involved with the individual child, thus considering his or her personal, social and emotional development as well as their academic attainment. This approach recognises that children have a range of needs and will require different forms and levels of support and guidance, including different approaches used to manage their behaviour. A child with behavioural difficulties will need clear boundaries, with the expectations for their behaviour made explicit to them. It is also important to be consistent so that they learn the positive and negative consequences of their actions. Children can easily become 'labelled' for their behaviour and it is important to challenge this view at every opportunity.

Example: *Jaspinder frequently gets into trouble in the playground at lunchtime. Instead of greeting him by saying, 'oh, not you again, Jaspinder, what have you done today?', try saying, 'gosh, Jaspinder, what has happened here? I am so surprised to hear that something has gone wrong in the playground today'.*

Do explain to the other children in the class what is happening and why, as well as how they can help this child without patronising him/her. Children generally respond better if they have been involved in devising and agreeing the strategies used to support their behaviour. Similarly, honest and clear communication with parents, if sensitively handled by a teacher, can encourage them to become active participants in this process as well.

Children sometimes get into difficulties in school because they do not understand school language, customs and rules. This might be because they are not familiar with it, for example, if they are new to the school system, if they have not been attending school regularly because they come from a family of 'travellers'. It is easy to take for granted the customs and culture of a particular school and fail to recognise the complexity of these for some children. So always explain the reasons for things carefully.

Finally, adopting an inclusive approach requires you to explicitly teach all children alternative ways of responding to challenging situations so that they can counteract stereotyping, bullying or harassment of any kind. This can be done very effectively through circle time, class discussions or assemblies. These approaches can also provide opportunities to explore the emotional component and/or the effects of stereotyping. Do not avoid discussing with children the damaging effects these issues can have on an individual's self-esteem. Drama is a safe and yet powerful way to explore these scenarios and emotions with children.

Reflecting and evaluating

The most important aspect of adopting an inclusive approach is recognising that this is a process and so you will need to continually reflect and evaluate the success of the strategies you are using within your teaching. These should ensure that you are meeting the needs of all children while also trying to offer them access to these challenging equal opportunities issues.

Preparation and task 1
Carry out an audit of the resources available in your classroom in terms of gender, disability, cultural/ethnic, linguistic and religious diversity.

Consider books as well as artefacts and other resources. Don't forget that other adults can share a great deal of expertise and become a valuable additional resource to support your teaching.

Evaluation and follow up
If you identify any areas of weakness and concern, how would you want to remedy this? What can you do to enrich the resources you use within your teaching and which are available for the children? (See the resources audit activity within the section on creating the learning environment.)

Task 2
Evaluate the strategies that you are using within your teaching to ensure equal access and opportunities. Use the headings below to structure your thinking. Suggest ways that you might improve one dimension under each heading.

Aspect of my teaching	How successful am I currently? Include evidence/examples of strategies currently being used	How am I going to improve this?
Interpreting the curriculum		
Employing inclusive teaching strategies		
Considering behaviour management		

Evaluation and follow up
For a couple of weeks try to focus specifically on each of the issues you have identified in the table above to improve one thing in each of the following aspects of your practice:

- ➲ interpreting the curriculum;
- ➲ employing inclusive teaching strategies;
- ➲ considering behaviour management.

Review and evaluate your progress. Discuss this with your teacher and gain their view of your progress as additional evidence of your development. Having tried to think about and incorporate some of these equal opportunities issues into your teaching, you should now be confident to evaluate your understanding of this aspect of your practice.

Your achievements

Now you have read this section and completed the activities you should be able to:

➲ consider and understand the implications for your practice of each of the principles of inclusion contained within the National Curriculum 2000;
➲ understand the wider context underlying the need to adopt inclusive practices in relation to ensuring that all children are provided with appropriate learning opportunities to achieve their best;
➲ understand and be able to use a framework for equal opportunities to inform your teaching;
➲ employ inclusive teaching strategies and continually evaluate these;
➲ consider your approaches to behaviour management and continually evaluate these;
➲ ensure that all the children in your class have equal access and opportunities;
➲ monitor and evaluate the success of your approach to this;
➲ audit resources in terms of gender, disability, cultural/ethnic, linguistic and religious diversity;
➲ use this information to improve the range of resources which you use to support your teaching.

If you feel that you have completed the tasks successfully, return to the relevant needs analysis and mark it off with the date and evidence. Ask your tutor about being able to use this activity as evidence that you have met the Professional Standards for QTS. Refer to the summary of Standards listed in the Appendix.

Now that you have reached the end of this chapter on developing your skills you should feel confident that you have had the opportunity to explore and practise some aspects of your professional knowledge, understanding and skills across all the themes covered. It is essential that you check that you have evidence to support all the statements within the needs analysis table at this level and that you have also cross-referenced this to the Standards required for QTS in the Appendix. Engaging in reflection and critical dialogue with your teacher is an important aspect of your learning and development at this stage. You will also need to ensure that you have started to complete the profiling required by your training provider since this may cover additional Standards.

Chapter 5   **Extending your Skills** ⤳ Introduction

Contents

The information and activities in this section are aimed at trainees who are at the last stage of their work in school and completing an extended final school experience. By this stage, you will be taking responsibility for planning, teaching and assessing the whole class for the majority of the teaching time. You will also be expected to take an increasingly active role in the life of the school community, attending staff meetings, helping with extra-curricular activities and so on. The expectation is that you will already have worked through the 'Developing your Skills' chapter and activities outlined earlier in this book.

The activities described can be carried out in a range of primary settings, with different age groups and, given that they are related to your general professional practice, can be completed within different subject teaching. For example, you can choose which subject areas you are going to locate the required activities within. You will need to link activities if you are also using the other subject-based books within this series. So do take advantage of the fact that the 'Professional Issues' activities can and should be linked to a range of different curriculum subjects. At this level the teaching activities are designed to be carried out with a whole class. However, others provide an opportunity for you to reflect on and consider the detail of your understanding of these professional issues at a deeper level so that you are equipped to enter the profession and take up responsibility for a class of your own.

For the purposes of auditing your development during your training you will need to refer to the Standards in DfES/TTA (2002) *Qualifying to Teach: Professional Standards for Qualified Teacher Status*. A summary version of the Standards that can be addressed during different themes is included as an Appendix at the back of this book. Please refer to this regularly. As you complete each piece of evidence that accompanies the activities it is important that you share this with your supervising teacher, school-based mentor and/or training provider tutor, as relevant. This profiling process is an important one but you should be given advice on this from your training provider. Do ensure that you link the completion of the activities in this chapter with the profiling requirements of your training.

The matrix below outlines the content and activities for this chapter. Each theme has been divided into six common elements. Use the summary of the Standards for the Award of Qualified Teacher Status in the Appendix to see how your experiences at this level can contribute directly to the profiling process.

	When finding out about policy and practice in the school	When observing other teachers' practice	When observing children	When planning for the class	When teaching a class	When reflecting on your teaching
How do you define yourself in the role of the teacher?	Ensure that you are adopting all the school's policies and practices in relation to parental partnership.	Complete an audit of the different professional roles and responsibilities that you have undertaken (formal and informal).		Contribute to shared activities with colleagues, e.g. collaborative planning, school assemblies, extra-curricular clubs, trips, etc. Identify the advantages and responsibilities associated with working as a member of a team.	Communicate effectively and appropriately with all the adults with whom you work.	Evaluate the communication systems and strategies in use by the adults in your classroom.
How do children learn and teachers teach?		Observe the teacher's use of different types of questioning; identify the types of questions being used, their purposes and effects.	When observing the teacher's use of questions, observe the responses of the children.	Plan activities that reflect a variety of learning styles.	Use a range of different types of questions for different purposes.	Evaluate the effectiveness of your use of questioning. Review the appropriateness of your teaching approaches in relation to the children's styles of learning.
How do you create a learning environment?	Discuss and agree behaviour management policy with colleagues. Read and discuss Health and Safety policy. Discuss structure of class timetable with teacher.			Plan and create displays which celebrate children's attainments and support learning.	Negotiate and take responsibility for the class timetable.	Review the success of your use of the behaviour management policy in the classroom.
How do you plan for learning and teaching?	Read the school's curriculum policies in any remaining subjects. Look at the long term planning and schemes of work relating to the key stage you are working in.			Devise a medium-term plan based on the school's long-term planning and schemes of work to include all subjects.		Review your medium-term planning and reflect on what you have learned about the planning process.
How do you assess and record children's learning	Get a copy of the school's annual Report form. Find out what support materials the school have available to support levelling children writing.			Plan a writing activity which will enable you to assess and level some children's attainment against National Curriculum level descriptions.	Annotate and level children's writing using National Curriculum level descriptions. Communicate effectively with parents in different ways about their children's progress.	Review what you have learned about using a 'best fit' model to level children's work. Review your understanding of the target setting process and the need to use data from a variety of sources on children's attainment to inform your teaching.
One school for all?	Read, discuss and understand the various relevant Statutory documents.		Anticipate and prepare to challenge children using inappropriate language and behaviour towards one another.	Take account of equal opportunities and inclusion issues in all your planning, teaching and interactions with children.	Consider two scenarios and identify how you would respond in each situation. Discuss these with your teacher.	Evaluate your practice against the key questions provided. Discuss this with the teacher and head teacher.

All the activities in this chapter are outlined in full and have the following information provided with them:

⊃ essential background to the activity including such items as which equipment to use and which setting might be most appropriate for carrying it out;
⊃ a description of the activity and all the elements which go to make it up;
⊃ ideas on how to evaluate its success;
⊃ suggested further background reading;
⊃ your achievements.

How do you define yourself in the role of the teacher?

Link to Professional Standards for QTS

Please refer to the Appendix for information about the links between this theme and the Professional Standards for the Award of Qualified Teacher Status.

Becoming a teacher

Being responsible for the daily running of a classroom is a complex job. With experience, many of the routines become second nature. For trainees and teachers wishing to remain reflective, a proactive approach is essential. Take positive steps to create a productive working environment and enhance the children's learning. This will probably include taking responsibility for new initiatives and projects. Trainees can bring new inspiration and energy to a school. Experienced teachers will benefit from the exchange of ideas and should support trainees who wish to take risks and enrich school life by getting involved in wider activities such as assemblies, clubs, trips, celebrations and sports days. At all times trainees should ensure that they are working within the policies and guidelines of the school, thus making best use of the available resources and providing protection and support when necessary.

Preparation
Read Hayes (1999) Chapter 12.

Task
Complete an audit of the roles and responsibilities you have undertaken whilst working in school. It may be helpful to divide these into formal and informal roles and responsibilities.

Evaluation and follow up
Identify which of these you were expecting and which have come as a surprise to you. You may wish to list other aspects of teaching which you would predict you will encounter in the future. Cross-reference these roles to the Professional Standards for the Award of Qualified Teacher Status.

Respectful relationships

In larger schools you may find that you are able to work with two or more teachers as part of a year group or Key Stage team. Although the teacher remains your principal partner, this can provide a further source of expertise and experience on which to draw. There are many advantages to working as a member of a team. Responsibilities and tasks can be shared, individual skills can benefit other members and it can provide a support network, essential in such a demanding job. With these advantages also come responsibilities. Work must be shared out equally and completed as agreed, you may feel you have less autonomy and flexibility having to accommodate the needs of others and there will be times when you have to compromise. As a trainee, establish your role within a team and be clear about your responsibilities.

As children approach major transitions, such as moving to the next class or from Key Stage 1 to 2 or from primary to secondary school, they will have concerns and expectations which will require the teacher to provide additional support and show extra sensitivity. These changes will have a significant effect on each child, as new relationships will need to be established and the security of the familiar is left behind. Careful planning, and specific arrangements, can address these concerns and help to ease the transition. It is worth remembering that confident children who are developing into responsible, independent people will cope better in these situations and their learning will be only slightly disrupted.

Relationships with parents can be an extremely positive force or a problematic area. Either way, it is undeniable that they are a vital element of the process of meeting children's needs. Many parents will want to discuss matters with teachers outside of formally arranged meetings. On a personal level, they may want to get to know the person who is responsible for their child's learning and well-being for so much time. Most parents will also want to know how they can contribute to their child's education and may have questions and problems they need to discuss. At all times a calm and professional approach should be taken. This will help to give parents confidence in you, make them feel involved in their child's learning and provide opportunities for delicate issues to be handled with sensitivity. School policies on home–school partnership encourage the development of positive relationships.

Preparation
Read Hayes (1999) Chapter 4.

Task
Collaborate with another teacher or as a member of a team to prepare for a future event. This may be the planning for the next half term, an assembly, running an extra-curricular club or organising a trip.

Evaluation and follow up
Identify the advantages of working as a member of a team or partnership. Evaluate your role in the team and how you helped the other member/s. Identify the ways in which the children benefited from the input of other teachers. Identify any problems you encountered or would predict might occur during future collaborative activities.

Successful communication

Successful communication within the classroom contributes to focused learning and positive working relationships. This learning is of limited use if it simply remains within the confines of the classroom and is never celebrated with others. Sharing children's achievements and overcoming challenges in partnership with parents is an important part of the process.

Primary schools provide an annual written report on each child, which is a summary of their progress and achievements during the year. There are opportunities for more personal exchanges during regular parents' evenings. Parents can see children's work and discuss their perceptions and any concerns they may have. As Hayes (1999, page 35) points out, 'every meeting with parents has the potential to enrich or inflame an existing situation'. There is much that can be done to ensure a positive experience for all. The classroom and children's work should be organised and ready for close scrutiny. Planning what you want to say to the parents and providing thoughtful, sensitive and honest responses to their questions will fulfil the expectations of the majority of parents.

Preparation
Read Hayes (1999) Chapter 3.

Review the school's policy and practices in relation to parental partnership. Discuss any issues arising with the teacher.

Task
Plan for and attend a parents' evening or meeting with specific parents. Give feedback on the child's progress, make sure you are well prepared and have notes, a photograph and information about the child and his or her achievements.

Evaluation and follow up
The teacher should be present during the meeting and can provide feedback and pointers for you to act upon next time, both in future parents' evenings and in less formal encounters.

Adult helpers in the classroom

Children will encounter adults fulfilling a range of roles within the school community. Moyles (1992, page 137) provides a comprehensive list:

- ➲ other teachers with a peripatetic role within the school;
- ➲ advisory teachers and advisors;
- ➲ other teachers with a subject-specific role;
- ➲ other teachers perhaps in parallel classes or adjacent classes;
- ➲ the head teacher or deputy (particularly if they are without their own class responsibility);
- ➲ supply teachers;
- ➲ people from outside agencies such as educational psychologists, speech therapists, a school nurse or children's librarian;
- ➲ instructors, such as bilingual or swimming instructors;
- ➲ home liaison personnel;
- ➲ nursery nurses;
- ➲ ancillaries or welfare assistants;
- ➲ school meals personnel and caretakers;
- ➲ parents/guardians and other relatives, e.g. grandparents;
- ➲ governors;
- ➲ specific visitors, e.g. a local artist or craftsman invited in for a particular purpose, police officers or fire officers;
- ➲ students (whether student teachers, nursery nurses, sixth-formers and/or those gaining work experience);
- ➲ college/university tutors;
- ➲ researchers;
- ➲ general 'visitors', perhaps teachers from other schools, overseas visitors and such like.

New adults should always be introduced by name to the class. They will usually be quickly accepted into the classroom community. Each of these people has a particular role to play. It is the teacher's job to ensure that best use is made of their skills and expertise. The presence of additional adults in the classroom can be a blessing, providing extra support and working with groups of children. It also requires careful management by the teacher. Children's learning can benefit enormously from individual adult assistance and children with special educational needs may be entitled to this support. Whenever adults are there to support the teacher, it is sensible to provide them with a plan of the lesson and useful information about their role. When they work closely with an individual or small group, assistants need to be involved in the overall monitoring of the children's progress. They may be in a position to provide insights into the children's achievements, although the teacher retains overall responsibility for assessment and reporting to parents.

Preparation
Read Moyles (1992) Chapter 6.

Observe the ways in which the teacher uses other adult support in the classroom. These may include teaching assistants, parents and other adults.

Task
Plan to make the best use of adult helpers during one of your lessons. Provide them with a plan and ensure that they are clear about their role during the lesson. Discuss the lesson with them afterwards and encourage them to feed back information about children's achievements and progress.

Evaluation and follow up
Evaluate the ways in which the use of other adults during the lesson supported children's learning. Identify ways in which you can improve and maximise this in the future.

Your achievements

Now you have read this section and completed the activities you should be able to:

➲ identify the range of roles involved in teaching;
➲ work as an effective member of a team;
➲ identify the advantages and responsibilities of being a member of a team;
➲ plan for building children's confidence;
➲ prepare for a parents' evening;
➲ provide parents with feedback about their child's progress;
➲ maximise the potential of the input of other adults in the classroom;
➲ communicate with other adults to inform you about children's achievements and misconceptions.

If you feel that you have completed the tasks successfully, return to the relevant needs analysis and mark it off with the date and evidence. Ask your tutor about being able to use this activity as evidence that you have met the Professional Standards for QTS. Refer to the summary of Standards listed in the Appendix.

How do children learn and teachers teach?

Link to Professional Standards for QTS

Please refer to the Appendix for information about the links between this theme and the Professional Standards for the Award of Qualified Teacher Status.

The ongoing challenge of learning and teaching

In the previous sections it has been argued that teaching should be based on evidence of what constitutes effective strategies. Some of this evidence will be from your direct experience of what works for the children in your class. But this alone is not enough. Your strategies should be informed by what we understand about how children learn.

Knowing what works for you

The process of learning to be a teacher is one in which you gradually come to understand what sort of teacher you want to be. You will have opportunities to observe and work alongside a range of teachers with different personalities, styles and teaching approaches. Some styles you will admire, others you may feel are not for you. Within the broad parameters of teaching that is 'fit for purpose' you will evolve your own style. Only you can decide the sort of teacher you want to be. You may try out different styles along the way, rather like trying on a different coat and seeing whether it suits you. Teachers often have to be actors. When you go into the classroom you take on a role, but you can only become the sort of teacher that you really want to be if the relationships, approaches and classroom you develop accord with your basic values. In order to become that teacher, you must remain open-minded to the possibility of gaining insights and learning new ways of doing things.

Continuing to develop your knowledge base

By this stage in your training you will already have given a lot of thought to current theories of learning and have observed and refined your own teaching in the light of these. To continue to develop your understanding you might like to read and reflect on the work of scientists and educationalists who have influenced thinking in education in recent years. In particular, research by Susan Greeenfield (2000, 2001) into the development of the brain has led to new understanding of how children learn. In terms of the curriculum, Colwyn Trevarthen's work (1997) on the social and cultural context of learning has influenced thinking in education. There are now some additional elements which influence the way children learn which you need to consider in order to focus and develop your teaching strategies.

Preferred sensory systems

Research into the way that individuals receive and process information indicates that there are three basic sensory systems at work: visual, auditory and kinaesthetic. The population divides into three roughly similarly sized groups, each of which has a preferred or dominant style. You may know instinctively which style you prefer. This does not imply that you only receive, process and remember information this way, merely that this is your dominant sensory system.

Visual learners are most successful when learning using pictures, diagrams, mind maps and so on. Auditory learners relate well to songs, rhymes, stories and music. The kinaesthetic learner is a 'doer' and learns well through role-play, movement and practical activity. Children and adults often reveal their preferred sensory style in the language that they use. The visual learner may use visual imagery and say things like 'That looks good to me' or 'I can see this will go well'. The auditory learner will say 'That sounds fine', 'I hear what you say' or 'I like the sound of that'. From a kinaesthetic learner you may hear comments like 'That will work out fine' or 'That will go well'. Listen to the conversations of the children in your class as they work together and you will hear remarks that indicate their preferred style. You should use this understanding when planning activities or grouping children for a particular task. You could try grouping together children with the same or differing dominant styles and evaluating the outcomes of their work.

In terms of the classroom the preferred sensory style is important for two reasons:

⊃ Bear in mind that approximately one third of your class will be visual, one third auditory and one third kinaesthetic in terms of their preferred sensory preference. Do you cater for all their styles in your teaching?
⊃ You also have a preferred style yourself and this is the approach that will suggest itself most readily when you are planning your teaching. Try consciously to reflect the other styles when you are planning. It can be helpful to plan with others who have a contrasting style to your own.
If you are interested in finding out more about the preferred sensory style of the children in your class and how to use this to support learning, you will find further information and a range of classroom activities in the work of Alistair Smith (1996, 1998).

In your regular evaluation of planning and teaching, make sure that you review the range of activities offered to the children. Does one sensory system dominate the activities and approaches you have adopted? What does this review tell you about the needs of the children in your class?

Developing your skills in questioning
In the previous section you were encouraged to think about your use of questions as part of your teaching strategy.

Forms of questions
In the classroom an experienced teacher will use a range of different forms of question, which each have a different purpose. Some examples of different purposes are:

⊃ focusing attention, with phrases like:
    can you see…
    did you notice… or
    what is …
⊃ comparing and classifying, by asking, for example:
    how many…
    how long… or
    what differences can you see or hear…
⊃ seeking clarification, with phrases like:
    what do you mean by …
    can you explain further…
    can you give another example of … or
    explain that another way…
⊃ inviting enquiry, with phrases such as:
    what do we need to know…
    how can we find out…
    what would happen if… or
    can you find a way to…
⊃ seeking reasons and explanations for example by asking:
    how do you know…
    is it always so…
    why do you say that… or
    what is the evidence for…

Preparation

When observing your class teacher, make a note of the range of questions she uses and their purpose. Record the information in the following format:

Type of question	Question asked and context	Purpose	Children's response
Focusing attention			
Comparing and classifying			
Seeking clarification			
Inviting enquiry			
			'
Seeking reasons and explanations			

Task

Look back over your observations and evaluate the success of your use of questions. How did the children respond? Did the question support or develop their understanding? When planning your next teaching activity use your observations as a checklist to plan some different types of questions. If this lesson is to be observed by your teacher, ask her to use a similar format to give you detailed feedback.

Evaluation and follow up

In your lesson evaluation focus in particular on your use of questioning, based on your perception or the teacher's feedback. Reflect in particular on whether your questioning supported or developed children's understanding.

Based on your reflection and evaluation, what will you do differently in the next lesson in this sequence? Make some notes on your medium-term or weekly planning sheets.

Ongoing learning and reflecting

However long you remain a teacher you will continue to learn, from colleagues, from parents and from the children themselves. Some of this new learning will come in a formal context, but much of it will happen informally, and arguably the most valuable learning may come about this way.

At the end of your PGCE course, whatever its structure, you will devise your career entry profile. This is a document, completed by you, which outlines your strengths and identifies areas for development as you begin your teaching career. You will take it with you to your first teaching post and it will form the basis of your induction year as a teacher, indicating the areas in which you feel your new head teacher and colleagues should provide support and training.

This support may come through formal training, provided by your local education authority or other agencies such as higher education institutions in your area. Most universities have a wide range of professional development courses, which may be funded or part funded from your school in-service training budget. Support and training may also be provided by support in the classroom from subject leaders, advanced skills teachers or advisory staff working for the local authority. LEA advisors, advisory teachers and curriculum consultants can be a useful source of information, professional support and contacts. There may be particular projects or curriculum development initiatives in which you can be involved once you have established yourself as a class teacher.

The other way in which you can continue to develop as a teacher is through your own reading and research, much as you have developed throughout your PGCE training. You should keep an eye on professional journals which find their way into the staff room, and perhaps subscribe to one or two in areas of particular interest. You need to make sure that you continue to find your own role models, observe others and reflect on your own practice. You may find that in a year or so it is students in training, placed with you, who are providing a valuable source of new ideas, much as you are doing now!

Your achievements

Now you have read this section and completed the activities you should be able to:

⊃ further develop your own style of teaching and understand what works for you;
⊃ recognise the influence of preferred sensory systems on how children receive, process and remember information;
⊃ provide a range of activities and teaching approaches which recognises this diversity;
⊃ recognise the way in which your preferred styles influence your teaching and the implications of this for your planning;
⊃ identify the purposes and effects of questioning when observing others teaching and when planning and teaching yourself;
⊃ use questions skilfully to elicit and probe children's understanding and support their learning;
⊃ evaluate children's learning in the light of your questioning;
⊃ reflect on the complex range of factors which influence how children learn.

If you feel that you have completed the tasks successfully, return to the relevant needs analysis and mark it off with the date and evidence. Ask your tutor about being able to use this activity as evidence that you have met the Professional Standards for QTS. Refer to the summary of Standards listed in the Appendix.

How do you create a learning environment?

Link to Professional Standards for QTS

Please refer to the Appendix for information about the links between this theme and the Professional Standards for the Award of Qualified Teacher Status.

Rules and routines

Schools will have a behaviour management policy explaining the ethos of the school and the particular strategies used in the classroom. These strategies will be most successful if every member of staff applies them consistently. Each school is different, but most schools employ a system of rewards and sanctions which work alongside some basic rules.

Establishing class expectations for behaviour, or 'golden rules', at the start of each year is an opportunity to ensure that every child understands what the rules are and why they are necessary. This process could be reviewed at the start of a period of school experience to familiarise the trainee with the rules, remind the children of the rules to which they agreed and help to establish the trainee in a position of authority. By involving children in this process, they will have some ownership of the rules and should be more inclined to keep to them and encourage others to do so. Children will also need to be reminded of the positive and negative consequences of keeping to the rules and failing to do so.

Preparation
Read Pollard (1997) pages 101–8 and Cowley (2001) pages 129–40.

Task
Discuss the behaviour management policy with the teacher. Make sure you are clear about the rewards and sanctions and discuss the golden rules chosen by the class. Apply these consistently in every lesson that you teach.

Evaluation and follow up
At the end of each of the first few weeks of the school experience review the strategies you are using with the teacher. Which rules are working well? Why is this the case? How do the rules help children to work? Which areas are causing problems? How can your strategies be adjusted to cope with these?

Timetabling

Each school day is complex. Some points on the class timetable will be fixed by school organisation, such as cross-class setting, the use of the hall or swimming lessons, but much of the time will be organised by the teacher. When making decisions about the length and order of lessons, there are several aspects to consider. A balance needs to be struck between varying activities in order to keep children's attention and moving from one lesson to the next so quickly that children do not have time to learn. A good timetable will provide a variety of activities with days broken down into chunks which are manageable for children.

Conversely, it is also important to consider what is being asked of children when they move from one lesson to the next. It can be difficult to be creative or logical on demand, so moving quickly from an art lesson to mathematics may not be easy. It will be necessary to clearly end one lesson and help the children to 'switch off' from the learning style. A simple device such as a change of seating arrangements or quick game, followed by a clear introduction to the next lesson, should help children to make the adjustment. Ideally lessons requiring very different teaching and learning styles should be separated by a break time to ensure that there is sufficient time to reorganise resources and prepare yourself.

The timetable should be clear to the children, so putting a copy on the class notice board will keep children informed. It is advisable to involve the children in some of the decisions about the timetable. At the very least, an explanation of why the decisions were made will help them to feel that they understand it and can work within it. Their opinions and ideas could then be elicited and acted upon if possible, to give them some ownership. This will enable them to take some responsibility for ensuring they have the correct resources for lessons and can help the teacher prepare for the day. It can also support those who need firm structures to work within, such as autistic children.

Preparation
Read Moyles (1992) Chapter 5.

Task
Examine and discuss the class timetable with the teacher. Establish which periods are fixed by whole school organisation and discuss why others are organised as they are. Make sure there is time to prepare for practical lessons, that resources will be available at the right time and that there are some quieter times built into each day. Discuss the flexibility of the timetable and negotiate any minor changes with colleagues and children. Make sure that all children are aware of the location of the timetable and are able to read it.

Evaluation and follow up
Review the timetable after a few weeks and revise where appropriate, focusing on the learning needs of the children and the organisation of lessons.

Managing the whole class

When you are teaching the whole class you will employ many of the management strategies you used with a group, but you will need to move around the classroom. You will be monitoring learning and behaviour in different groups. This is necessary even when you are focusing on one group or individual. You may be managing more than one activity within a subject or having different subjects going on at the same time. This involves careful planning, organisation and communication but can be a very efficient and effective way of organising learning. Techniques such as carefully organised partnering can help the children to work through problems together and they will learn a great deal through this process. The planned use of learning support assistants and other adults working in the classroom can help to keep children focused and maintain an effective learning environment for all.

There are many strategies for establishing and maintaining a purposeful working atmosphere. Every teacher has his or her own techniques and you will need to develop a set of strategies which you find effective and comfortable. Different lessons will have different working atmospheres, from silence to noisy and busy activity. You may want to define a variety of working styles and use signs, signals or spoken indications of which is suitable for specific lessons or activities, for example 'quiet mice' for near-silent individual work and 'busy bees' for interactive work involving discussion and movement.

You will need to decide what level of noise and activity suits your teaching style and each lesson that you teach. Some lessons, such as science investigations or collaborative map work, will require children to discuss and interact and will therefore be noisier and more active than lessons employing more traditional methods of learning and teaching such as handwriting or observational drawing. When using potentially dangerous equipment, perhaps during PE or design and technology, noise levels will need to be reduced in order for a safe environment to be maintained.

Planning and classroom organisation must take account of those children who complete work early and require consolidation or extension activities. Similarly you will need to consider those children who may not complete work during a lesson and decide whether completion of the work is necessary to ensure they have met the learning objectives. To ensure that all of these children are able to work independently, resources need to be organised in such a way that children can access what they need without disturbing the flow of their learning. Keeping children informed about the amount of time they have for an activity will help them to take more responsibility for their own learning. Some teachers use a system of traffic lights to signal how much time is left to complete work to encourage children to concentrate and put their energies into appropriate tasks.

Preparation
Read Jacques and Hyland (2000) pages 80–9.

Task
Examine planning from the previous term, make a note of the different groups used and discuss these with the teacher. Establish what groupings are used in different subjects and how this supports children's learning.

Evaluation and follow up
Evaluate the advantages and disadvantages of whole class, group and individual work based on your own teaching experiences and observations of other teachers.

Resources

You will need to have an overview of planning for each term to ensure that appropriate resources are available and visits or trips organised well in advance. Access to shared resources should be considered at the point of medium-term planning. Ensure that you identify the resources you will require in order to create a stimulating learning environment. This will include rooms, ICT equipment and audio-visual materials to name only a few. It is vital to establish what is available in school and what you will need to organise from other sources such as the LEA library service, museums, toy libraries and resource centres. You will need to meet with colleagues and subject leaders to discuss when you will need the resources and who else will need access to them, as planning may need to be altered to take account of this.

Many classes have the support of a learning support assistant for some time during each week. The other adults who support you in the classroom form a valuable resource. In order for them to contribute to the learning environment fully, assistants should be given opportunities to contribute to planning and bring their own resources to teaching. Other adults including visitors can also be used as resources. Parents, community nurses, ministers of religion, dentists and police officers have experience which can be utilised to enrich the learning environment and widen children's perceptions of school and learning.

At the start of term clear one or two display boards and prepare them with backing paper or fabric for a new display. Consider how to make best use of the different display areas inside and outside the classroom in relation to the planning for the term. Displays contribute to the learning environment by celebrating children's work, providing motivation, information and stimulating discussion and investigation. Displays should vary in style and content, including text, images, children's work, posters, books and equipment. How frequently you change the displays needs careful consideration and should relate to planning. Schools usually have a display policy, detailing styles of presentation and labelling. This is useful for inexperienced teachers for whom constructing displays is a new skill; however, you will develop your own style and ideas as time progresses. The content and style of classroom displays will depend to a large extent on the learning needs of the children in the class.

Preparation
Read Hayes (1999) pages 74–76.

Task
Plan for the creation of two displays using contrasting styles. Explain to the children that some or all of the work from this activity is to be included in the displays to encourage good quality work. Prepare the display boards or areas with suitable backing, labels and resources. Mount and display children's work and discuss the display briefly with them.

Evaluation and follow up
How do the children react to the display? How do they interact with the materials and each other? How are the displays used over a longer period of time?

Health and safety

Children's safety is of paramount importance and, as the teacher, you are responsible for the children in your class. Every school has a health and safety policy with which you should familiarise yourself. The policy will contain preventative measures which should be taken and procedures for coping with problems if they occur. For example, whenever a child is hurt in an accident it should be recorded in detail in the accident book. Keeping a record of events is always necessary to ensure that information is available should there be longer-term effects. Accidents of a serious nature may have to be reported to outside agencies such as the LEA.

As well as the classroom there are other spaces around the school which constitute parts of the children's learning environment. These should be put to good use and you will need to ensure that children are properly supervised wherever they are working. Unsupervised children may be in danger and will be unlikely to achieve learning objectives. Good use should be made of learning support assistants, parents, library staff and other adults. Similarly, use of outdoor areas such as playing fields, playgrounds, ponds and conservation areas needs careful planning and safety issues should be carefully considered in order to ensure children's safety and a positive learning outcome. Children may need to be organised into smaller groups with a greater number of adult assistants, almost as if the children were going on a school trip.

Preparation
Read Moyles and Robinson (2002) Chapter 17.

Task
Read the school health and safety policy. Make sure you are clear about aspects which may affect work in your classroom such as fire drill procedures, the identity of staff with responsibility for first aid and the location of the accident book.

Evaluation and follow up
Consider what preventive measures should be taken to avoid accidents and what you will do in the event of an accident occurring while you are responsible for the class.

Your achievements

Now you have read this section and completed the activities you should be able to:

➲ familiarise yourself with a school behaviour management policy and recognise its importance;
➲ use established school and class routines and rules to establish a purposeful working atmosphere;
➲ evaluate the effectiveness of class rules and start to develop your own strategies for managing the class;
➲ recognise the need for varied activities during the day in order to maintain children's concentration and maximise learning opportunities;
➲ negotiate and take responsibility for the class timetable;
➲ plan and use different groupings according to learning objectives and activities;
➲ provide and organise resources that encourage independence;
➲ organise creative, stimulating displays and evaluate their effects on children's learning;
➲ familiarise yourself with a school health and safety policy and take pre-emptive action to avoid accidents in the classroom.

If you feel that you have completed the tasks successfully, return to the relevant needs analysis and mark it off with the date and evidence. Ask your tutor about being able to use this activity as evidence that you have met the Professional Standards for QTS. Refer to the summary of Standards listed in the Appendix.

How do you plan for learning and teaching?

Link to Professional Standards for QTS

Please refer to the Appendix for information about the links between this theme and the Professional Standards for the Award of Qualified Teacher Status.

The planning process

You have already planned individual lessons and sequences of lessons. This section goes on to look at more integrated medium- and long-term planning. It is sometimes difficult for trainee teachers to get experience of long- or medium-term planning because this may well be in place when you join the staff on school experience. Because planning has to be progressive across the school, it is often difficult to change it for one class or year group as changes in one class or year group may have implications for teaching elsewhere in the school.

However, the process of planning itself, especially collaborative planning with colleagues, is a powerful support for teaching. It is much more meaningful for you as a teacher to work from your own or shared planning – you know the thinking that has gone into it, the needs of the children you are planning for and you fully understand what you are trying to achieve. Taking 'ready-made' solutions off the shelf is never the same – this is not your planning, it has not been constructed based on the particular circumstances of your school and your class, it does not recognise the particular strengths and expertise available to you.

This is not to devalue the material available to support the planning process in your class, year group or school. You may find that these documents are a useful source of ideas and resources that you can draw on. Creating your own medium-term plans provides the opportunity to develop cross-curricular links which, it is argued, are the most effective way of providing a coherent curriculum for primary age children.

Example: *A Year 6 teacher has planned a project linking work in science, mathematics, English, design and technology, art, ICT, music, history and PSHE. There is a patch of ground outside the classroom which is damaged by children who regularly ride their bikes over it at the weekend. The children design a garden which they will plant and develop here, based on research they have undertaken. Budgeting for the cost of tools, plants and benches is done using a spreadsheet. They work with elderly people in the community to develop a historical theme for the garden, based on the former industrial heritage of the area. These ideas are expressed in a clay mosaic which is to be incorporated into the design. They write to local people, organisations and businesses to raise funds and appeal for materials for the project. They invite local politicians and business people to a presentation evening at the school at which they entertain their guests, present the project and seek support. Younger children in the school are involved in the project both by being consulted and by being encouraged to take care of the garden during an after-school club.*

Changing and refining planning

Sometimes, even when long-term planning has been agreed throughout the school and schemes of work have been developed based on this planning, changes have to be made in order to meet the needs of individual classes or particular situations. Year groups of children vary both in terms of class dynamics and levels of attainment. The opportunity to take part in a special programme, for example, such as an artistic residency, theatre visit or an innovative ICT project, may require changes to the long- and medium-term planning. Any such changes must always be discussed with colleagues because they may have implications for the work of other staff.

Educational visits and special projects provide unrivalled opportunities to enrich children's learning experiences, but these may not be without difficulty. Extensive planning is needed both to maximise the value of the visit and to ensure its safety and smooth running. In addition, some children may not be able to participate if their parents are unwilling to give consent. Although schools and LEAs are sometimes able to offer financial support if that is the reason for the parents' unwillingness to allow their child to take part, sometimes consent is withheld for reasons of culture, religious belief or safety. This has important implications for curriculum planning.

Example: *At Woodside Primary School the Year 6 children have a chance to go on a residential visit to an outdoor pursuits centre run by the local authority. At the centre the children will have opportunities for exciting work in science, geography and history, take part in canoeing, walking and abseiling, as well as benefit from living together as a community for the week. Despite the best efforts of the school to include everyone in this experience, some parents are unwilling to let their children take part, and generally about five to ten of the children in the class are not included. Not only does the class teacher have to plan to make the most of this valuable learning experience for the majority, she has to be sensitive to the feelings and learning needs of the other children and cater for their needs too in the preparatory work and follow-up.*

At its best, a good primary curriculum is based on:

➲ long-term planning that ensures coverage of the National Curriculum, with continuity and balance between the subjects being taught;
➲ medium-term planning that ensures breadth and progression in children's learning, with a meaningful context in which they can develop as learners, and which links to the National Curriculum programmes of study;
➲ short-term planning which identifies learning objectives, focused teaching, interesting activities, assessment opportunities and differentiation.

Preparation
Look at the long-term plans and school's schemes of work covering the year group you are teaching for the time period you are in school. This is the material that you will be expected to cover whilst you are teaching the class. Discuss with the teacher any issues that might influence the planning on this occasion and make sure you are familiar with the policies relating to all of the subjects you will be teaching.

Task
Based on the requirements of these documents, produce a medium-term plan to cover the period of your school experience. Assuming that most of the literacy and numeracy teaching is planned discretely, you can still include English and mathematics in your medium-term plan. In this way you can look for opportunities to apply and develop the use of English and mathematics across the curriculum. Identify formal assessment opportunities as part of your planning. The issue of planning for assessment is discussed in more detail in the following section. Link your planning to the programmes of study of the National Curriculum and the National Literacy and Numeracy Strategies. Decide which aspects of the work can be linked in a cross-curricular topic or theme and whether any will have to be covered discretely.

Evaluation and follow up
Having completed your medium-term plan, discuss it with your teacher and then plan the first week of your teaching in detail, including clear learning objectives, differentiation and the use of ICT.

At the end of your first week of teaching, review the remainder of your medium-term plan and make adjustments to it accordingly. Look back over the planning process you have been through and discuss it with your teacher.

C5 Planning

Your achievements

Now you have read this section and completed the activities you should be able to:

➲ create your own medium-term plans for teaching in all subjects of the curriculum, based on the school's long-term planning;

➲ respond to the needs of your class, or particular opportunities that may arise, when interpreting the long-term plan and producing your medium-term planning;

➲ produce medium-term plans which ensure breadth and progression in children's learning and a meaningful context for their learning to take place;

➲ produce weekly planning and lesson plans with clear learning objectives, interesting and challenging activities and which recognise children's individual needs;

➲ identify formal assessment opportunities at the stage of medium-term planning;

➲ create opportunities for children to apply and develop their skills and understanding in English and mathematics across the curriculum;

➲ create opportunities for children to develop thinking and problem-solving skills and creativity;

➲ create opportunities for children to develop their personal, social and cultural understanding across the curriculum.

If you feel that you have completed the tasks successfully, return to the relevant needs analysis and mark it off with the date and evidence. Ask your tutor about being able to use this activity as evidence that you have met the Professional Standards for QTS. Refer to the summary of Standards listed in the Appendix.

How do you assess and record children's learning?

Link to Professional Standards for QTS

Please refer to the Appendix for information about the links between this theme and the Professional Standards for the Award of Qualified Teacher Status.

Essential information

This section will enable you to extend and deepen your understanding of some other features of the assessment, monitoring and recordkeeping process so that you develop a coherent approach to this within your own practice.

Understanding the levelling process

The process of levelling children's work to provide an indication of how their attainment compares with the 'expected norms' or range of performance possible from children at that stage in the learning is one which you will need to practise in order to become proficient. Although this should really be done at the end of each Key Stage, it is common practice now for teachers to carry out this process on a regular basis in order to monitor children's performance and set new targets for their learning. This is also closely related to the high levels of accountability of teachers for the progress of the children in their class.

Having selected a piece of work to level, this should first be annotated. This annotation should provide information about the date, context in which the piece of work was completed, the amount of support or help which was provided and an indication of the specific nature of this help. Then reference should be made to the relevant attainment target which would relate to the piece of work.

Example: *If this is a numerically based piece of mathematics work, refer to mathematics attainment target 2: number and algebra. If this is a piece of science work about living animals, refer to science attainment target 2: life processes and living things.*

The attainment targets identified in the example above refer only to the subject content of the work. You may also wish to level the 'process skills' demonstrated by the child, in other words how they went about that piece of work. This might involve their ability to engage in scientific enquiry, in which case you will also need to refer to the appropriate attainment target for that aspect. This would be science attainment target 1: scientific enquiry. Similarly, a piece of scientific writing could be used to assess the level of writing which a child is doing, in which case you would need to refer to the English attainment target 3: writing.

Children's expected level of attainment is set out in the different level descriptions in each subject of the National Curriculum. Try to decide which one level 'best fits' the pupil's performance. This will then be the level that is allocated to this piece of work. Before confirming your judgement make sure that you refer to the description for adjacent levels to check the accuracy of your judgement. It is also important to take into account what you as the teacher already know about that child. So if there are aspects of that level not evident in this particular piece of work, you may already have evidence that the child has demonstrated those aspects or might need to collect that evidence on a subsequent occasion. Be confident to use other assessment strategies to support the collection of this additional information.

Target setting

The process of setting targets, monitoring progress against these and reviewing them is an additional feature of the assessment process which has been introduced into schools over the past few years in order to raise standards of attainment. Targets can be both numerical and curriculum related depending on what kind of target they are and their purpose. There are many different types of target set and these can be:

➲ national targets;
➲ local education authority targets;
➲ whole school targets;
➲ Key Stage targets;
➲ class targets;
➲ group targets;
➲ individual targets.

At this stage in your training you need to be aware of the process of target setting and why it is a feature of school practice but you need only really concern yourself with setting and using individual and class targets within your own practice. It is always important to talk to and learn from colleagues who have responsibility for these procedures in school such as the head teacher or the assessment co-ordinator.

As with other aspects of assessment, targets are useful only if they directly inform your planning and teaching and are an explicit feature of your work with the children in your class. To achieve this they need to be displayed, referred to frequently and reflected within your feedback and marking to the children. To support children in achieving their targets, provision for working towards these must also be present within your planning. The most effective targets are likely to be set by those who are involved in achieving them, which requires the teacher and children to work together. This need for children to feel some ownership to their learning and the link between this and their motivation and self-esteem has already been discussed in earlier sections (**page 30**). The targets also need to be understandable for children, with a clear indication of how they will know when they have achieved them, and so they will usually be SMART targets, which have already been discussed.

Reporting on achievement to parents

Pollard (1997) describes two contradictory sets of expectations which influence the reporting process to parents. The first sees parents as partners in their child's education with an equal but different role to teachers and thus needing to be kept informed of the detail of their child's progress, performance and development in school. This is usually achieved through informal day-to-day interactions and parents' meetings which often happen on a termly basis. The second assumption is based on a model of parents as consumers of education and thus the school is accountable to them for the quality of their provision, as measured through the pupils' performance. This is why schools need to keep parents informed of pupils' achievements and results. The provision of annual reports on children is a statutory requirement and these need to contain information about general progress, including the child's attendance record. They also contain comments on specific progress within each subject area of the National Curriculum or learning areas for those children in the foundation stage. If relevant, information on statutory assessments should also be included (for Year 2 and 6 children). Schools will also make explicit the arrangements for a parent-teacher discussion of the report if this is required. Some schools ask parents to make a written comment on their child's report each year.

If any of these reporting processes occur while you are training in a school, it will be valuable for you to join in and contribute to these. This is an important opportunity to learn how to conduct discussions with parents and find out about 'what to do and what not to do' before you are responsible for a class of your own.

Preparation and task

Collect detailed information on two children in your class and compile an annual report to their parents using the report pro forma provided in the school. This is a simulation and the report should **not** be presented to the parents. Instead show it to your teacher and discuss the detail of the content with him or her.

Evaluation and follow up

Evaluate what you have learned through this process and ask the teacher if you might see some reports that other teachers have completed on children. These might need to be 'anonymised' to protect the confidentiality of the children, teacher and parents.

Preparation

Plan a task for your class which requires them to complete a piece of narrative writing. Ensure that you provide them with the required support so that they can succeed at this task. This might include establishing an interesting focus for the writing or using a story to stimulate their thinking but perhaps changing the ending. It depends on the age of the children you are working with as to what would be appropriate support. It might just include providing them with sharp pencils, line guides and paper with a margin already drawn.

Task

Now mark the writing and choose three pieces to evaluate and level more carefully. These should be from a high attainer, a middle attainer and a low attainer. Annotate the work to identify clearly the support that was provided for each of the three children when doing this task. Now use the National Curriculum level descriptions as well as any additional guidance materials which may be available to the staff in the school in which you are working to level the work as accurately as you can.

Ask two teachers working in the age groups either side of you if you can look at the written work of three of their children. Again select a piece of narrative to focus on and ensure that they have given you a representative piece of work from the three attainment bands in each of the two classes. So if you are working in Year 4, you should now have your three examples of writing from your own children, three from Year 3 and three from Year 5 to work with. Lay out the writing in a matrix form as below and evaluate it in the manner described below.

Year 3	Year 4	Year 5
High attainer's work	High attainer's work	High attainer's work
Middle attainer's work	Middle attainer's work	Middle attainer's work
Low attainer's work	Low attainer's work	Low attainer's work

First look down the work in each column respectively. This should clearly indicate different levels of attainment. Is there any evidence of the high-attaining child writing well, the middle-attaining child doing reasonably well but writing less and the low-attaining child not finishing their work? If this is so, what might you want to do about it? What explanations might there be for this?

It probably indicates that the task was not appropriate or that some children were not given the correct amount of support since all the children should have completed the task successfully. Next view the work across each row in the matrix and think about how each piece of work represents a year's progression. Start with the high attainer and then look back to the example from the previous year and the one for the following year. Do these give you a better view of how children can progress and what your expectations might be? Compare this to the content of the relevant level descriptions in English for writing. Repeat this process for each attainment group.

Evaluation and follow up

What have you learned about how to level children's work accurately and the whole process of identifying progression in learning from year to year while locating this within the levels of the National Curriculum? Discuss with your teacher and the assessment co-ordinator in the school the other procedures used for sampling and moderating children's attainment within and across year groups. Also find out from them what procedures are in place within the school for using this information to set individual targets for children.

Now that you have completed this final section of work on assessing and recording children's learning you should feel confident that you understand the procedures for carrying this out. You will also have had the opportunity to consider some of the strengths and limitations of different assessment strategies that can be used to collect this information. The key point is that assessment should be used to directly inform future planning. You need to act on the information gained to modify your practice or the teaching approaches you are using or alter the curriculum or a combination of these aspects.

Now you have read this section and completed the activities you should be able to:

⊃ understand the levelling process and use this to judge the attainment of the children in your class across different areas of the curriculum;

⊃ understand the target-setting process and how this can be used to raise the standards of attainment of the children in your class;

⊃ use the target-setting process to directly inform your teaching of individuals, groups and the whole class;

⊃ consider the issues related to reporting to parents and know how to provide this information verbally and through annual written reports;

⊃ mark and level children's writing using the National Curriculum and then use this information to evaluate the range of attainment within the class;

⊃ compare levelled work across the attainment range from three different year groups and use this process to inform your understanding of progression;

⊃ consider the implications of this process and act upon the information gained to inform your teaching.

If you feel that you have completed the tasks successfully, return to the relevant needs analysis and mark it off with the date and evidence. Ask your tutor about being able to use this activity as evidence that you have met the Professional Standards for QTS. Refer to the summary of Standards listed in the Appendix.

Chapter 5   One school for all?

Link to Professional Standards for QTS

Please refer to the Appendix for information about the links between this theme and the Professional Standards for the Award of Qualified Teacher Status.

Essential information

'Wherever we come from, whatever our roots, or our faith, we have a stake in being British and we can be proud of that. Celebrating diversity and building a fairer, more confident multicultural nation with a fresh, strong sense of national identity is an important and timely project. Having confidence in yourself and holding on to a dream of what you can achieve is so important. Nothing should hold you back in reaching your full potential. I want a society that gives you these chances, a society where each of you, regardless of colour or race or religion, has an equal opportunity to succeed. It is your future and we need to hear from you.'

The Home Secretary speaking to black teenagers, 17 March 1999 (quoted on page 7 in Raising the Attainment of Ethnic Minority Pupils – guidance and source materials for initial teacher trainers)

It is very important that as a trainee you are aware of the array of legislation that directly affects the work you are doing as a teacher. There are a number of important Acts which you will need to take account of as you perform your professional responsibilities. Here are some of the key ones and you are referred to additional reading in order to explore the detail of these (see the Bibliography on **page 125**):

- ➲ Sex Discrimination Act 1975;
- ➲ Race Relations Act 1976;
- ➲ Disability Discrimination Act 1995;
- ➲ Health and Safety at Work Act 1974;
- ➲ Children Act 1989;
- ➲ DfEE Circular 10/95 Protecting Children from Abuse (1995).
- ➲ Special Educational Needs and Disability Act (2001).

As well as ensuring that you incorporate equal opportunities (and inclusion) issues into your planning for the curriculum and the learning environment, you will need to be prepared to challenge specific examples of inappropriate behaviour in your own class as well as elsewhere in the school. It is much easier to have anticipated and prepared for these rather than rely upon your instinctive response when the moment arises. Consider what you will do and say in the following instances:

- ➲ You overhear children using names such as 'fatty', 'thicky', 'specky'.
- ➲ A boy in the class refuses to sit or stand beside another because they are a 'girl'.
- ➲ Children make racist comments such as 'Paki', 'you don't belong here', 'chocolate face'.
- ➲ Children ask you, 'why don't they have to go to assembly?' when referring to some children who are Jehovah's Witnesses.

It is also very important that you take a proactive approach to equal opportunities issues. Ensure that your teaching always takes account of these and maximises the children's learning and understanding of these issues.

Example: *If you are working with young children and are acting out the following song, why not choose a female doctor? This selection will provide the chance to assess the children's responses. If they show any sense of surprise, use this as an opportunity to discuss their expectations.*

Five little monkeys bouncing on the bed, one fell off and bumped his head. Mother called the doctor and the doctor said, 'No more monkeys bouncing on the bed'.

Four little monkeys (repeat song going backwards to three, two and then one little monkey).

There are some excellent stories which can be used to trigger these kinds of discussions and learning (see Letterbox Library catalogue).

Do also ensure that you avoid exemplifying stereotypical behaviour yourself by saying 'I need a big strong boy to help me move this' or drawing attention to gender unnecessarily, such as lining up boys and girls separately. There are many other interesting ways of organising and dismissing the children from the class. Refer to the theme of organising the learning environment for further suggestions of these (see **page 77**). If you have ever experienced any kind of discrimination or racism yourself you may wish to share this and your feelings about it with the children, if appropriate.

Task
Consider the following scenario faced by a head teacher. Make a list of the key issues and then briefly describe how you would have responded to these parents.

A new Asian family has joined the school. The father has been working locally in the community for several years but the mother and the two children (Ayesha who is seven and Rahim who is nine) have just come to England. Neither of the children speaks very much English, although they are fluent in Urdu. About two weeks after they join their classes a few extremely articulate parents from Ayesha's class come to talk to you. They are concerned about the fact that the class have to take their Key Stage 1 national tests shortly and the other children in the class may perform below their ability because the teacher will have to keep stopping to explain the work more carefully to Ayesha. They are also rather worried that the teacher will begin to set easier work for the whole class because of Ayesha.

Evaluation and follow up
Show this scenario and your written response to the teacher you are working with and then discuss it with them. It would also be valuable to arrange to have a meeting with your head teacher and ask whether you could discuss these issues. Has he or she ever had any similar experiences to the one described in the scenario? How did they deal with them?

Ask them for their advice about the kinds of issues they think you need to be prepared to deal with in relation to equal opportunities and inclusion.

Task
Read the list below and evaluate yourself and your current practice against each of the following points:

- ➲ Do you believe that there are benefits to having a heterogeneous classroom?
- ➲ Do you understand that an inclusive education cannot be achieved by treating all pupils in the same way?
- ➲ Are you open to improvising in the classroom?
- ➲ Do you try to remain flexible and respond to the reactions of individuals within the class?
- ➲ How familiar are you with different cultural customs, beliefs and practices?
- ➲ Do you incorporate a range of resources, artefacts and stories into your teaching which represent positive images of disability, gender and ethnicity?
- ➲ Have you consciously tried to establish a caring ethos in which there is respect for one another?
- ➲ What strategies do you use to ensure that an environment is created in which children are confident to share experiences and talk about their feelings?
- ➲ Do you have high expectations for all the children in the class and refer to these explicitly?
- ➲ Do you plan with all the other adults working in your classroom?

➲ What strategies do you use to communicate with and ensure that all the adults working with and alongside you have the opportunity to contribute to the planning?

➲ Do you continually review all aspects of your practice and change these if necessary?

Evaluation and follow up

Ask the teacher/mentor with whom you are working to carry out the above review on your practice. Now arrange to discuss any discrepancies/similarities in both evaluations of your practice against the list of questions above. Do any surprises result from this discussion? Prepare an action plan for yourself to address/ improve one or more aspect of your practice in relation to the list above. This may be set out as below.

Area to be addressed	Action to be taken	Review period	Evidence of change

Your achievements

Now you have read this section and completed the activities you should be able to:

➲ understand the significance of a range of relevant statutory acts and be familiar with their content;

➲ always challenge stereotypical, racist or sexist remarks or behaviour manifest by children you work with;

➲ take a pro-active approach to equal opportunities issues and ensure that your teaching always takes account of these;

➲ imagine how you might respond to parents who are challenging aspects of school life on the basis of their prejudiced attitudes;

➲ discuss openly with your colleagues the issues related to equal opportunities and use these discussions to inform your thinking, understanding and teaching approaches;

➲ review and evaluate your beliefs and practice in the light of equal opportunities issues;

➲ devise an action plan to address/improve any aspects of your practice, based on this review.

If you feel that you have completed the tasks successfully, return to the relevant needs analysis and mark it off with the date and evidence. Ask your tutor about being able to use this activity as evidence that you have met the Professional Standards for QTS. Refer to the summary of Standards listed in the Appendix.

Chapter 5   **Extending your Skills** ➲ Conclusion

Now that you have reached the end of this section on extending your skills you should feel confident that you have had the opportunity to practise, refine and enhance your professional knowledge, understanding and skills across all the themes covered. It is essential that you check that you have evidence to support all the statements within the needs analysis table at this level and also that you have cross-referenced this to the Standards required for QTS in the Appendix. It is always helpful to engage in reflection and in critical dialogue with your teacher. You will also need to ensure that you have completed the profiling required by your training provider since this will cover additional Standards. This should equip you for your future in teaching and allow you to enter the profession with confidence.

Chapter 6   Moving on

In the introduction, views of what makes a successful primary teacher were used to identify the themes contained within this book. At this point in your training it would be helpful to return to these views and evaluate yourself against these attributes. This process of critical reflection underpins successful practice and creates teachers who are self-aware. It is one of the characteristics that the authors hope this book has nurtured and should now be a natural element of the way you work.

Now that you are approaching the end of your initial teacher training course, it is important for you to clearly identify your individual strengths and areas for further development within your professional practice. This is the start of a continuing process which is designed to support your professional development throughout your career. It will encourage you to set high expectations for yourself and continually update and improve your practice.

At the end of your training course you will need to reflect on your achievements to date. This will also require you to enter into a dialogue with your teachers and training provider tutors. The result of this process will be the completion of your career entry profile (CEP) in consultation with your training provider. The CEP will be used throughout your induction year to review your progress and drive the agenda for your continuing professional development. At the end of your induction year you will be assessed by the head teacher against the induction standards and you will also have to demonstrate that you have continued to meet the Standards for the Award of Qualified Teacher Status in an employment context.

You need to be clear about the arrangements for your induction period in terms of the procedures, the levels of support available to you and your roles and responsibilities. The details of these are available in the booklet 'Into Induction' (TTA, 2001) as well as on the TTA website.

The evidence you collect throughout this year can be used to begin your professional development record. This should record your progress, performance and professional development needs, which will be reviewed on an annual basis through the performance management process. This process is one aspect of a DfES initiative to encourage and support teachers in continuing to update and share their knowledge, skills and practice in order to enhance children's learning. The DfES has provided a framework which maps the different standards that apply at different stages of a teacher's career. It also includes ten dimensions of teaching and leadership which exist within a school and you are encouraged to chart your progress against these as you move through your career. It is important for you to recognise your areas of expertise and achievements as well as identifying your development needs. The dimensions are:

- knowledge and understanding;
- planning and setting expectations;
- teaching and managing pupil learning;
- assessment and evaluation;
- pupil achievement;
- relations with parents and the wider community;
- managing your own performance and development;
- managing and developing staff and other adults;
- managing resources;
- strategic leadership.

The DfES has recognised the need to support teachers who are in the early stages of their careers. There will be an early professional development scheme which is specifically directed at teachers in their second and third years of teaching. This will continue to provide support and training opportunities for you as you progress along your career path. We wish you every success on this journey.

Bibliography

How do you define yourself in the role of the teacher?

Bruner, J S (1990) *Acts of Meaning*. Cambridge, MA: Harvard University Press.

Fisher, J (2002) *Starting from the Child*. Buckingham: OUP.

Fisher, R (1995) *Teaching Children to Learn.* Cheltenham: Stanley Thornes.

Galton, M, Simon, B and Cross, P (1980) *Inside the Primary Classroom*. London: Routledge and Kegan Paul.

Hayes, D (1999) *Foundations of Primary Teaching* (2nd edition). London: David Fulton.

Kyriacou, C (1991) *Essential Teaching Skills*. Oxford: Blackwell.

Moyles, J (1992) *Organizing for Learning in the Primary Classroom*. Buckingham and Bristol: Open University Press.

Moyles, J and Robinson, G (2002) *Beginning Teaching: Beginning Learning in Primary Education*. Buckingham: Open University Press.

Pollard, A, Broadfoot, P, Croll, P, Osborn, M and Abbott, D (1994) *Changing English Primary Schools? The Impact of the Education Reform Act at Key Stage One*. London: Cassell.

TTA (2002) *Standards for the Award of Qualified Teacher Status*. London: TTA.

Vygotsky, L S (1962) *Thought and Language*. Cambridge, MA: MIT Press.

Websites
General Teaching Council for England – www.gtce.org.uk

Teacher Training Agency – www.canteach.gov.uk

How do children learn and teachers teach?

Bruner, J (1966) *Toward a theory of instruction*. Cambridge, MA: Harvard University Press.

Bruner, J (1986) *Actual Minds, Possible Worlds*. Cambridge, MA: Harvard University Press.

DfEE (1998) *The National Literacy Strategy – Framework for Teaching.* London: DfEE Publications.

DfEE (1999) *The National Numeracy Strategy – Framework for Teaching Mathematics from Reception to Year 6.* London: DfEE Publications.

DfEE and QCA (1999) *The National Curriculum Handbook for Primary Teachers in England Key Stages 1 and 2*. London.

Gardner, H (1993) *Frames of Mind: The Theory of Multiple Intelligences* (2nd edition). London: Fontana Press.

Greenfield, S (2000) *Brain Story: Unlocking Our Inner World of Emotions, Memories, Ideas and Desires.* London: BBC Worldwide.

Greenfield, S (2001) *The Private Life of the Brain*. London: Penguin.

Jacques, K and Hyland, R (2000) *Professional Studies: Primary Phase*. Exeter: Learning Matters.

Papert, S (1993) *Mindstorms: Children, Computers, and Powerful Ideas* (2nd edition). Brighton: Harvester.

Piaget, J (1926) *The Language and Thought of the Child*, New York: Basic Books.

Piaget, J (1961) *A Genetic Approach to the Psychology of Thought*, 52, pp. 151–61.

Pollard, A. (1996) *Readings for Reflective Teaching in the Primary School*. London: Cassell.

Pollard, A (1997) *Reflective Teaching in the Primary School – A Handbook for the Classroom* (3rd edition). London: Cassell.

Smith, A (1996) *Accelerated Learning in the Classroom*. Stafford: Network Educational Press.

Smith, A (1998) *Accelerated Learning in Practice: Brain-based Methods for Accelerating Motivation and Achievement.* Stafford: Network Educational Press.

Tizard, B and Hughes, M (1984) *Young children learning: talking and thinking at home and at school*. London: Fontana.

Trevarthen, C (1997) 'The Curricular Conundrum: Prescription versus the Comenius Principle.' Address to the Forum on Preschool Education in Scotland, Jordanhill, January.

Vygotsky, L S (1962) *Thought and Language*. Cambridge, MA: Massachusetts Institute of Technology.

Vygotsky, L S (1978) *Mind in Society: The Development of Higher Psychological Processes.* Cambridge, MA: Harvard University Press.

How do you create a learning environment?

Cowley, S (2001) *Getting the Buggers to Behave*. London: Continuum.

Hayes, D (1999) *Foundations of Primary Teaching* (2nd edition). London: David Fulton.

Jacques, K and Hyland, R (2000) *Professional Studies: Primary Phase*. Exeter: Learning Matters.

Kyriacou, C (1991) *Essential Teaching Skills*. Oxford: Blackwell.

MacGrath, M (2000) *The Art of Peaceful Teaching in the Primary School*. London: David Fulton.

Moyles, J (1992) *Organizing for Learning in the Primary Classroom*. Buckingham and Bristol: Open University Press.

Moyles, J and Robinson, G (2002) *Beginning Teaching: Beginning Learning in Primary Education*. Buckingham: Open University Press.

Pollard, A (1997) *Reflective Teaching in the Primary School – A Handbook for the Classroom* (3rd edition). London: Cassell.

How do you plan for learning and teaching?

DfEE (1998) *The National Literacy Strategy – Framework for Teaching*, London: DfEE Publications.

DfEE (1999) *The National Numeracy Strategy – Framework for Teaching Mathematics from Reception to Year 6*. London: DfEE Publications.

Hayes, D (1999) *Foundations of Primary Teaching* (2nd edition). London: David Fulton.

Jacques, K and Hyland, R (2000) *Professional Studies: Primary Phase*. Exeter: Learning Matters.

Kyriacou, C (1991) *Essential Teaching Skills*. Oxford: Blackwell.

Moyles, J and Robinson, G (2002) *Beginning Teaching: Beginning Learning in Primary Education*. Chapter 6. Buckingham: Open University Press.

Pollard, A (1997) *Reflective Teaching in the Primary School – A Handbook for the Classroom* (3rd edition). Chapter 7. London: Cassell.

QCA (1998) *Curriculum Guidance for the Foundation Stage*. London: QCA.

QCA (1998, 1999, 2000) *Schemes of Work for Key Stages 1 and 2*. London: QCA.

Website

www.skillsfactory.com

How do you assess and record children's learning?

Askew, M, Brown, M, Johnson, D, Rhodes, V and Wiliam, D (1997) *Effective Teachers of Numeracy – Final Report*. London: King's College.

Assessment Reform Group (1999) *Assessment for Learning: Beyond the Black Box*. University of Cambridge.

Black, P and Wiliam, D (1998) *Inside the Black Box*. London: King's College.

Bruner, J (1966) *Toward a Theory of Instruction*. Cambridge, MA: Harvard University Press.

Ebbutt, S (1996) 'Assessing numeracy' in R Merttens (ed.) *Teaching Numeracy: Maths in the Primary Classroom*. Leamington Spa: Scholastics Ltd.

Fisher, J (2002) *Starting From the Child* (2nd edition). Buckingham: Open University Press.

Gardner, H (1993) *The Unschooled Mind: How Children Think and How Schools Should Teach*. London: Fontana.

Gipps, C (1994) *Beyond Testing*. London: Falmer Press.

Gipps, C and Stobart, G (1993 or 1990) *Assessment: A Teachers' Guide to Issues*. London: Hodder and Stoughton.

Headington, R (2000) *Monitoring, Assessment, Recording, Reporting and Accountability. Meeting the Standards*. London: Fulton.

Holt, J (1982) *How Children Fail* (2nd edition). Harmondsworth: Penguin.

Lindsay, G (1998) 'Baseline assessment: a positive or malign initiative?' in Norwich, B and Lindsay, G (eds) *Baseline Assessment: Practice, Benefits and Pitfalls?*. Tamworth: NASEN.

Mitchell, C and Koshy, V (1993) *Effective Teacher Assessment: Looking at Children's Learning in the Primary Classroom*. London: Hodder and Stoughton.

Novak, J D and Godwin, D B (1984) *Learning How to Learn*. Cambridge: Cambridge University Press.

OFSTED (2000) *The Annual Report of Her Majesty's Chief Inspector of Schools: Standards and Quality in Education 1999–2000 Primary Schools*. London: HMSO.

Pollard, A (1997) *Reflective Teaching in the Primary School* (3rd edition). London: Cassell.

SCAA (1997) *KS 1 & 2 Assessment Arrangements*. London: DfEE.

Task Group on Assessment and Testing (1988) *Three Supplementary Reports*. London: DES.

Websites

Pupils' records and reports: DfEE Circular 0015/2000 – www.dfes.gov.uk/circulars

Teacher help web page for SATs – www.qca.org.uk/ca/tests/teacherhelp/

Standards reports on the 2001 Key Stage 2 tests – www.qca.org.uk/tests/standardsmain.asp

One school for all?

Blair, M and Bourne, J with Coffin, C, Creese, A and Kenner, C (1998) *Making the Difference: Teaching and Learning Strategies in Successful Multi-ethnic Schools*. London: DfEE.

Booth, T, Ainscow, M, Black-Hawkins, K, Vaughan, M and Shaw, L (eds) (2000) *Index for Inclusion:*

Developing Learning and Participation in Schools. Available from Disability Equality in Education or CSIE.

Cole, M (ed) (1999) *Human Rights, Education and Equality*. London: Falmer Press.

Commission for Racial Equality (2002) – www.cre.gov.uk/duty/duty.facts.html

Cowley, S (2001) *Getting the Buggers to Behave*. London: Continuum.

Cox, T (ed) (2000) *Combating Educational Disadvantage*. London: Falmer Press.

Daniels, H and Garner, P (eds) (1999) *The World Yearbook of Education – Inclusive Education*. London: Kogan Page.

DfEE (1995) *Protecting children from abuse*. Issue 10/95. London: HMSO.

DfEE (1999) '*Youth Cohort Study: The Activities and Experiences of 16 Year Olds: England and Wales 1998*.' Issue 4/99. London: HMSO.

DfES (2001) Statistics of Education: SEN in England. Bulletin, January (ref 12/2001).

DfES (2001) Special Educational Needs Code of Practice and Toolkit.

DfES (2001) Inclusive Schooling, Children with Special Educational Needs.

Frederickson, N and Cline, T (2002) *Special Educational Needs, Inclusion and Diversity*. Buckingham: Open University Press. (Part 1 is particularly useful.)

Gilborn, D and Gipps, C (1996) *Recent Research of the Achievement of Ethnic Minority Pupils*. London: Ofsted/HMSO.

Gilborn, D and Mirza, H (2000) *Educational Inequality – Mapping Race, Class and Gender*. Report for OFSTED. London: HMSO.

Hayes, D (1999) *Foundations of Primary Teaching* (2nd edition). London: David Fulton.

Hill, D and Cole, M (eds) (2001) *Schooling and Equality: Fact, Concept and Policy*. London: Falmer Press.

Hodgetts, J (1996) *Equal Opportunities: A Resource Pack for Schools*. Wolverhampton: Dialogue.

Jacques, K and Hyland, R (2000) *Professional Studies: Primary Phase*. Exeter: Learning Matters.

Kyriacou, C (1991) *Essential Teaching Skills*. Oxford: Blackwell.

MacGrath, M (2000) *The Art of Peaceful Teaching in the Primary School*. London: David Fulton.

Mason, M and Rieser, R (1994) *Altogether better*. Comic Relief. London: Hobsons Publishing.

Moyles, J (1992) *Organizing for Learning in the Primary Classroom*. Buckingham and Bristol: Open University Press.

Moyles, J and Robinson, G (2002) *Beginning Teaching: Beginning Learning in Primary Education*. Buckingham: Open University Press.

Murray, P and Penman, J (eds) (2000) *Telling Our Own Stories: Reflections of Family Life in a Disabling World*. Published by Parents with Attitude, P O Box 1727, Sheffield S11 8WS.

Pollard, A (1997) *Reflective Teaching in the Primary School*. London: Cassell.

OFSTED (1998) Recent Research on Gender and Educational Performance. University of Cambridge/OFSTED. London: HMSO.

OFSTED (1999) *Raising the Attainment of Minority Ethnic Pupils – Schools and LEAs' Responses*. London: HMSO.

TTA (1999) *Raising the Attainment of Ethnic Minority Pupils – Guidance and Source Materials for Initial Teacher Trainers*. Letterbox Library (71–73 Allen Road, London N16 8RY, tel: 020 7503 4801).

Websites

Alliance for Inclusive Education – www.allfie.org.uk

British Dyslexia Association – www.bda-dyslexia.org.uk

Centre of Studies for Inclusive Education – http://inclusion.uwe.ac.uk

Commission for Racial Equality – www.cre.gov.uk

DfES Inclusion website – http://inclusion.ngfl.gov.uk

Disability Equality in Education – www.diseed.org.uk

Disability Rights Commission – www.drc-gb.org

ENABLE – Network, 40 poor world countries for inclusion – www.eenet.org.uk

Parents for Inclusion – www.parentsforinclusion.org

Appendix

This details the links between the themes covered in this book on professional issues and the Professional Standards for Qualifying Teacher Status.

The Standards for the Award of Qualified Teacher Status are outcome statements that set out what a trainee teacher must know, understand and be able to do to be awarded QTS. The Standards are organised in three inter-related sections which describe the criteria for the award.

Professional values and practice
These Standards outline the attitudes and commitment to be expected of anyone qualifying to be a teacher and are derived from the Professional Code of the General Teaching Council for England.

Knowledge and understanding
These Standards require newly qualified teachers to be confident and authoritative in the subjects they teach and to have a clear understanding of how all pupils should progress and what teachers should expect them to achieve.

Teaching
These Standards relate to skills of planning, monitoring and assessment, and teaching and class management. They are underpinned by the values and knowledge covered in the first two sections.

How do you define yourself in the role of the teacher?	
Standards covered across all levels within this theme 1.1, 1.2, 1.3, 1.6, 1.7 2.4, 2.7 3.3.1, 3.3.7, 3.3.9	
Additional standards covered related to each level	
Getting Started	
Developing your Skills	1.6, 3.1.4
Extending your Skills	1.4, 1.5, 1.8, 3.1.4, 3.3.11, 3.3.13

How do children learn and teachers teach?	
Standards covered across all levels within this theme 1.1, 1.2, 1.3, 1.6, 1.7 2.2, 2.3, 2.4	
Additional standards covered related to each level	
Getting Started	
Developing your Skills	
Extending your Skills	

How do you create a learning environment?

Standards covered across all levels within this theme 1.1, 1.2, 1.3, 1.7 2.4, 2.7 3.1.3, 3.1.5, 3.3.1, 3.3.5, 3.3.7, 3.3.8, 3.3.9	
Additional standards covered related to each level	
Getting Started	
Developing your Skills	1.4, 1.6
Extending your Skills	1.5, 1.6, 3.1.5, 3.3.11, 3.3.13

How do you plan for learning and teaching?

Standards covered across all levels within this theme 1.1, 1.2, 1.3, 1.6, 1.7 2.2, 2.3, 2.4, 2.7 3.1.4, 3.3.1, 3.3.3, 3.3.4, 3.3.5, 3.3.7, 3.3.9	
Additional standards covered related to each level	
Getting Started	
Developing your Skills	3.1.1, 3.1.2
Extending your Skills	3.1.1, 3.1.2, 3.1.5, 3.3.5, 3.3.6, 3.3.11, 3.3.13

How do you assess and record children's learning?

Standards covered across all levels within this theme 1.1, 1.2, 1.3, 1.7, 1.8 2.2, 2.4 3.2.1, 3.2.2, 3.2.4, 3.3.1	
Additional standards covered related to each level	
Getting Started	
Developing your Skills	1.4, 3.1.1, 3.1.2, 3.2.7
Extending your Skills	1.4, 1.5, 3.1.1, 3.1.2, 3.2.3, 3.2.5, 3.2.6, 3.2.7, 3.3.6, 3.3.11, 3.3.13

One school for all?

Standards covered across all levels within this theme 1.1, 1.2, 1.3, 1.4, 1.6, 1.7, 1.8 2.2, 2.4, 2.5, 2.7 3.3.1, 3.3.4, 3.3.6, 3.3.9, 3.3.13, 3.3.14	
Additional standards covered related to each level	
Getting Started	
Developing your Skills	3.1.1, 3.1.2, 3.1.3
Extending your Skills	1.5, 3.1.2, 3.1.3, 3.2.4, 3.2.5, 3.3.5

Index